Marcus Stobbe

SOLUTION-ORIENTED COMMUNICATION
... and the smile returns

The ABC of Changes

1st Printing 2003

This book is sold subject to the condition that it shall not, by the way or otherwise, be lent, re-sold, hired out, or otherwise circulated without the publisher's prior consent in any form of binding other than in which it is published and without a similar condition including this condition being imposed on the subsequent purchaser

Copyright © Marcus Stobbe, 2003
All rights reserved

ISBN 3-8330-0101-1

Herstellung: Books on Demand GmbH

INDEX

Introduction	7
I. A Christmas Tale	10
II. Introductory words to discuss a problem	14
1. Invitation to discuss a problem	17
2. Non-verbal acknowledgement	23
3. Questions to behaviour	25
4. Questions about thoughts	31
• Changes of inner rules by SATIR	
• Re-structuring of thought by MEICHENBAUM	
5. Questions about emotions	36
6. Circular questions –	40
Enquiry into the view of other important people	
7. Dissociation	45
• De-focussing	
• Questions for coping	
8. Transition to solution-orientation	48
III. Introductory words to discuss a solution	54
9. Questions to goals and future	63
• Miracle question	
• The 'to do as if'-question	
• Table of decision	
10. Scale questions	74
11. Questions about successful exceptions of the problem	80
12. Questions about reserves and abilities	83
13. Questions about the next step	87
14. Compliments and helpful questions	91

15. Exceptional forms of communication — 94
    - Paradox Communication
    - Provocative Communication
    - Exaggeration
    - I-Communication by Gordon
    - The 'coffee-chat'

16. Departure to solution-orientation — 105
    - The critical dialogue by Ellis
    - Rephrasing

17. Exercises for weekdays — 114
    - Prognosis-task
    - 'To do as if' task
    - Benefit-task

18. Final questions — 118

19. Lead-in to the next discussion — 121

IV. 10 Mistakes and how to avoid them — 132

V. 10 Questions and 10 Answers — 143

VI. Literature — 147

INTRODUCTION

Throughout their lives people's personality develops through positive solving of current conflicts. Sometimes upcoming problems may motivate, now and then they seem to be insuperable hurdles, such that we lose faith in our actions and therefore do not even perform them.

In 1952 EYSENCK established that any action would lead to a significant improvement. It is far more efficient to confront conflicts and do something rather than to complain and not change anything at all.

This book will give you the methodical tool, to replace current problems with practical solutions: solutions you carry inside yourself! You will learn a number of questions put in a certain order; questions you can put to yourself or to a partner. These are complemented by scientifically checked methods that proved useful within the private and professional everyday life.

> *Learning is like rowing against the current. As soon as one stops, one will be driven back.*
>
> BENJAMIN BRITTEN

As each person has lived through individual experiences and each deem other questions or methods effective for oneself, there are three possibilities of changes for nearly every question: A, B or C. For each structure there will be three different options, offering the basics for conversations and at the same time enabling individual phrasings. Within this book you will find space to develop your own questions and tips how to use them for answers regarding your current topic. This book will be a valuable companion venturing the departure to new shores within the world of solutions. This book tries to clarify that the questions herein are sufficient to get along on your own way to solution, with whatsoever problem might show up.

Part 1 of the book, problem conversation, deals with the detailed comprehension of situations one experiences as problems.

Some say – it is not easy to talk about problems. But especially in Germany people tend to chat about their problems more than anything else, also remarking that one can do nothing about them.

If one listens to two persons on i.e. a bus, who are relating their sorrows, one can observe that they do not help each other with questions, but both only relate their own problems. In this form of conversation people do not listen to each other and the support is lesser than it could be.

But would it not be nicer, to support the partner? Though intuitive advice is mostly rejected, i.e. saying: "That won't work!" or "I've already tried everything!"

> Nothing is given more generous than advice and there is nothing that should be more restrained.
>
> FRANZ VI, Duke of La Rouchefoucauld

Well, if extraneous solutions will not help, maybe your partner can activate his/her own results from the past. The solution-oriented dialogue will help your partner to visualize the desired condition and to recognise and use his/her own resources to reach his/her goals.

Searching for your own abilities and reserves, the success and the conscious planning of steps towards a goal, are the topics of this book. They will help you, as well as fulfilling your own solutions, also to arouse the solution-orientation of your partners.

What I have got to say is not unknown. It has proven worthwhile and can be looked up in books of various authors. What is new is only the compilation of proven methods to a constructive whole that led my partners and me to leave the lethargy in a problem and to strive for solutions and reach goals more lively. The joy of solutions created my energies to describe this way comprehensibly, such that everybody can master it like the alphabet. As much as I am interested in solutions, the first step towards them is a proper look into the current situation including the accompanying thoughts, feelings and behaviour.

Part 2 of the book, solution conversation, offers a whole host of questions and methods to comprehend solutions. You can use those questions:

- to develop your personality and reach your goals/visions,
- to mediate disputes with friends or relations,
- to lead successful discussions with co-workers, superiors and customers.

The chapters contain suggestions, exercises, a case example and a check list. Latter was compiled to integrate techniques into the personal style of thoughts and communication. The modus operandi is classified in a Christmas Tale, wherein Santa Claus's helper saves Christmas for the children with solution-oriented thinking.

I would like to thank my colleagues and friends here, Ursula Zenses, Oliver Röse and Frank Alexander, the book would look different without their ideas.

Nettetal, January 2003
Marcus Stobbe

I. A CHRISTMAS TALE

Once upon a time, whilst checking the packed sleigh, Santa Claus said to his helper:
"You know, I don't think I'll be able to get all the presents to the children on time this year. I'm getting old, my race-moose would rather do moose-tests then pull the sleigh and the presents also get bigger and bigger …"

"Hmm, Boss," his helper nodded. For several hundred years he'd called Santa Claus Boss. They were a good team with allocated roles.

The helper was responsible for wrapping the presents, packing the sleigh, planning the routes and times as well as choosing the fastest sleigh and race-moose.

Years ago he had swapped the reindeers for moose, whose power and stamina in pulling the sleigh had been fantastic and still were.

His boss was responsible for contacts to the children and the decision which gift should be bought for a child. Oh yes, not to forget he was also responsible for their mutual Christmas activities, meaning that all complaints were directed to him, sometimes making him sad and unenthusiastic.

Santa Claus carried on, "And when the complaints come in, especially for CDs, where one cannot tell the difference between techno-songs and others, then I'm answerable. That's not so nice. And the children's mode of expression nowadays, well I could tell stories …"

"What are you thinking about, Boss?" his helper asked, as he knew his boss' moods.

"Well I do ask myself for whom am I doing all this! I want to stay in my bed of clouds and nibble my Manna. As long as I don't have to open any mail after Christmas. I already dread it at this minute."

"How would you describe your feelings on opening the mail?" the helper asked nosily, as he was very interested in his partner's feelings.

"That's not so easy, I cannot really …, one should not really …, one shouldn't talk …, but if you ask me …" Santa Claus stammered and took a deep breath. "I then feel alone and helpless and ask myself whether or not I made mistakes and if I might not be too old for this job!"

"What would the children say, if they saw you lying down up there?" the helper enquired.

"Ooh they'd say this man has worked throughout his life, he's lost interest, he's too old for the job, he should retire or at least bring the proper gifts."

"Oh yes," his helper thought, "I know about the problem, but it's time to get away from this mood!"

He then shouted enthusiastically: "Look boss, the clouds are clearing and we can fly down to Earth in this beautiful sunshine. Isn't that a fantastic view!" He was well aware that sometimes it was necessary to pull his boss out of his mood and he thought the time was just right, as he knew his boss' feelings. Santa Claus face brightened, he looked down to Earth and said:

"Oh look, that's Sweden down there, where we had to change the moose some years ago. Yes, I remember it clearly! We then had that new sleigh, that ran so smoothly around bends."

"Don't you think, Boss, that we should do our round again this year as always?" the helper asked.

"Go on your own, you can do it as good as I can. Do it for me!" Santa Claus said leaning against the sleigh (exhaustedly).

The helper had not expected this. A lot of thoughts came up: On his own? To the Earth and back? And in the meantime? Gifts from the helper instead of Santa Claus? All the tales would have to be rewritten. Who should inform the parents? And how should they tell their children? He was not happy about the thought to be solely responsible for the Christmas gifts. At first he wanted to say:

"I've got my own work every year, I can't manage everything!" or "Can't you send someone else?" up to "Then I'll stay here as well!" But then he realised what he really wanted to do: Like every year he wished to bring happiness to the children over Christmas as a team with his boss. Therefore he took a different route to open his boss' eyes about the nice sides of the job.

He said: "Boss, think about the children down on Earth last year. Remember how they looked on opening the gifts on Christmas Day."

Santa Claus thought about this for a while and recalled many pictures: Yes, the children's eyes were glistening under the Christmas Tree, there were ahs and ohs, red cheeks and cuddles for the parents. They cuddled each other and the children shouted: "Thank you dear Santa Claus!" Santa Claus smiled.

"Did you hear music there?" the helper carried on.

"Oh yes, my favourite song: *White Christmas*, sung by Frank Sinatra!" replied Santa Claus enthusiastically. He started to whistle the tune. His helper even thought he had seen Santa Claus make a few steps, as if he wanted to dance.

"Tell me Boss, on a moose scale of 1 to 10, 10 moose meaning you're making the children on Earth happy and can listen to Frank Sinatra, and 1 meaning none of this will happen. Where are you at the moment?" his helper asked.

Santa Claus thought about this for a moment and then replied: "Seven and a half moose!"

"Aha," said his helper and thought: that's already a lot, "have there been any situations, where you felt similar but were able to organise it successfully?"

Santa Claus had to think for a while, as he had had a long active life with many successes: "A lot, a lot," he murmured, "a short while ago for example, must have been around 1910, during a terrible onset of winter, I had to really pull myself together. I put on three coats, rubbed moose grease onto my body and off I went!"

"I'm impressed, how you coped with the cold, Boss, not everyone would have been able to," his helper said.

"Yes," Santa Claus said "looking back it was rather brave to risk this hard trip. Four moose did not survive, but I arrived on time at the children's homes and brought a lot of pleasure and happiness."

"You really pushed through to arrive on time. It must have been very hard. My compliments, Boss! Did you reward yourself afterwards?"

"As far as I can recall, I took a hot trip out of the sky to the Teufelsberg in the deep South. There was no manna but a devilish good shish-kebab – and it was wonderfully warm there!"

"Which of your abilities, skills and reserves, dear Boss, would you use to get a step higher on the moose scale and closer to the happy children and Frank Sinatra?" the helper asked.

"Well, it's not as cold this year, but punctuality is still important to me. I can hardly arrive a day later!" rumbled Santa Claus. "If only the mail wouldn't be there after Christmas!"

"What if the mail would be answered after Christmas without causing you trouble?" his helper thought aloud.

"Oh that would be a lovely Christmas present." Santa Claus considered, whilst the two of them started to harness the moose.

"Boss, just imagine", said the helper, "I'll come back from my well-earned holidays in three weeks and you've managed everything: the children's mail is done, without troubling you. You'll be totally relaxed and had a wonderful time instead. What will you tell me, how you managed it?"

A smile crossed Santa Claus' face, whilst he thoughtfully repeated: "I've already managed it you say and can lie down with my manna. I am relaxed and think about the lovely children. Hmm, well then I did not read the nasty letters! Someone else opened and answered them, I'll be given the nice ones to reply, the others have been dealt with by my helpers. I then only have to sign the friendly reply letters. Yes, that's good. But who could help me, ... who would be so friendly ... of course, why didn't I think of it earlier, the Angels! On the basis of their professional belief they can't refuse my request. And with their pure soul, they won't get angry, but will forgive the children!"

"Super Boss," said the helper "now you re really close to your wonderful goal to make the children happy. Do you need anything else to fulfil your goal?"

"Yes," said Santa Claus "that you get onto the sleigh, otherwise we'll be late. I'll inform the Angels on my return! Gee up!"

P.S. Since Santa Claus' helper spread solution-oriented thinking in heaven, the Angels have more diversion and the work is distributed equally amongst all wings. Each year after Christmas Santa Claus enjoys his manna and gives autographs.

And his helper? His helper took leave for two years, to act as advisor to the humans, to bring them pleasant visions and to assist them in the fulfilment.

II. INTRODUCTORY WORDS REGARDING THE DISCUSSION ABOUT PROBLEMS

A discussion about problems or difficulties can take many forms. Two supplementary forms are the conversation about problems and solutions.

A discussion about problems mostly takes place prior to the discussion about solutions and holds two purposes:

- to let somebody feel that he is understood and esteemed (establish a relationship),
- and to get a picture of problematic situations including emotions, feelings, thoughts and behaviour.

The central element of every dialogue about problems is the detailed understanding of problematic situations. Four abilities are necessary to accomplish this: to be able to listen, to emphasise non-verbally (wordlessly), to avoid perceptive mistakes and to use questions regarding thoughts, emotions, feelings, behaviour and the point of view of other important persons (circular questions).

The discussion about problems doesn't serve to analyse the cause or even diagnose. It is rather important to respect the client's need, that he has to explain and justify him/herself and the listener, why he enlists help. Besides, clients use their part of the conversation to describe the problem and are also convinced that the advisor can help more effectively the better he understands the problem. ... To act differently would mean to offend him/her (BAMBERGER, 1999). Some clients show a rather more problem-oriented than solution-oriented mind.

Problem-focussing means one's mind remains in a world of problems, repeating them and through this develop a pessimistic view towards solutions. At the same time former unpleasant feelings and emotions show up. Problem-orientation can be recognised in phrasings and actions that focus on the problem instead of the solution!

Verbal indications of problem-orientation involve:
- repetition of the problem,
- negative choice of words – 'awful', 'no chance', 'bad',
- negative descriptions – 'everything is going round and round in circles',
- undue generalization – 'nothing will ever change',
- self-reproaches – 'I'm too stupid',
- fears, thoughts of disaster – 'I will totally fail' or
- missing answers to solution-oriented questions.

> Don't condemn the sky, if you've suffered an accident, but bent your head and have a good look at your soul.
>
> FROM ARABIA

The following example shows how problem-orientation can affect somebody: If problem-oriented people find out that they ride 'a dead horse' in their job or private life, meaning that they no longer identify themselves with their surroundings, their job or relationship, they react as follows:
- They say: "We've always ridden the horse that way",
- They found a team to analyse the horse,
- They compare various dead horses,
- They change the criteria indicating that the horse is dead,
- They always talk about their dead horse.

Instead of intensifying the problem – the 'dead horse' – it would be more useful as well as more pleasant to change the line of vision and look into the future.

Solution-orientation means the vigorous struggle for goals in a good mood. Problems are regarded as daily events, as an agreeable challenge to be sorted out. This is possible if one releases ones thoughts from the unpleasant side effects of the problem and concentrates on the pleasant sides of the successful solution.

A wise saying by the Dakota Indians:
"If you notice you are riding a dead horse, jump off."

What is the success of solution-orientation? You experience the answer if your thoughts and actions as well as your conversations are solution-oriented, as described in Chapter 9. You can experience in yourself how your motivation and energy are activated to strive for and accomplish your goals. At the same time you can use the questions to arouse the energy of your clients by leading solution-oriented dialogues.

II. 1. INVITATION TO DISCUSS PROBLEMS

1A What is on your mind? What concerns you?
1B What would you like to begin with?
1C Please outline a concrete situation?

Most people wish to explain their problems first. Only thereafter they are ready to look at possible solutions. Therefore it is important to test our ability to listen. You will learn that concentrated listening, thinking and discussing over a longer period is not easy!

Check yourself:
Watch the news and then give a faultless summary. Faultless means: you did not forget anything right (mistake type 1) nor added anything wrong (mistake type 2). Our own feelings, needs, goals and memorised experiences lead us to evaluate things thus making the second mistake. We have to overcome these difficulties if we really want to listen. It is important for you to listen carefully to get a first picture with regards to topic, persons involved and difficult situations and to create a comfortable atmosphere. In case your client does not start talking about his problem you can open the topic.

∼

1A What is on your mind? What concerns you?

I would like to explain this question with a case example, involving an external coach and an executive (Mr. Smith) who have had several meetings over some time.

CASE EXAMPLE 1A

Coach: "Hello Mr. Smith! Nice weather today, isn't it!"
Mr. Smith: "That's right. One should be outside!"
Coach: "What would you like to discuss today?"
Mr. Smith: "Well, how shall I put it, I've got problems with my boss. He's extremely harsh."

It is up to you, your mood and your evaluation of the partner to decide in which form you will open the discussion. There are many openings to a discussion; but you should avoid negative ones like "What bothers you? What is your problem?" or anything alike. It is more important that the listener can gather and see what the actual topic is:

- Is there an internal problem – Has your partner difficulties with him/herself?

- Is there a problem in a relationship – Has your partner problems with other people?

- Are you getting confused – You cannot follow his/her dialogue?

Noticing this you should take notes, even if it is a chat between friends. Your dialogue would be more professional, i.e. all important information is written down and you will avoid any mistakes of Type 1 and 2. Especially in the professional aspect, e.g. in meetings, it is more efficient for decision making and acting, if a record of important information is maintained. Inattentiveness and a repetition of questions because responses were not memorised would be interpreted as missing esteem.

It is better to work through one topic instead of several: to reduce the complexity, therefore do request your partner to concentrate him/herself on the topic that is most important.

After the partner had the opportunity to reveal what is on his/her mind to let the internal agitation out (certainly during the first conversation), request him/her to determine the topic he/she wants to discuss today.

∼

1B   What would you like to begin with?

CASE EXAMPLE 1B

Mr. Smith: "… first he (superior) ignores me, then I'm harassed and put at a disadvantage! And in the end I'm the fool!"
Coach: "There now, one after the other. Which topic do you wish to begin with?"
Mr. Smith: "Well, I'm under the impression that I get harassed! I won't take this much longer!"

The partner's decision determines the topic. If you do not know each other yet, it is possible that at first a minor problem is mentioned, as the partner wants to test your ability of discussion. A lot of people need proof of your competence before they give an insight of themselves and trust you. Friends, relatives and good acquaintances will immediately outline their most important matters, as a good relation as well as the atmosphere of openness and trust already exists. Bit by bit the openness will increase, if the partner feels, that you are really listening and can dive into his world.

> One can often ease ones pain when relating to someone.
>
> PIERRE COMEILLE

1C   Please outline a concrete situation?

It is important that you can get a picture of the situation as it supports your empathy and also reveals clues to what factors might inhibit or encourage the solution of the problem.

CASE EXAMPLE 1C

Coach: "You say you feel harassed. Can you please outline a concrete situation when you felt harassed?"

The question for a concrete situation, whether it's a problematic situation or a question about the successful exception of the problem, is one of the most important questions in the behavioural repertoire.

By reconstructing successful exceptions of a problem, the motivation to solve it can be built up. The reason for that is in the way something is stored in our memory. Experience is memorised in the form of pictures due to chemical changes and can be excellently recalled as pictures on the situations like a film clip. During a recall the stored thoughts, feelings and way of behaviour are also activated, although a subjective filter 'colours' the experience individually. Only if you enquire after the details of such situations will you get a clear picture in your mind from the beginning to the end and can avoid any distorted perception and judgement.

Which distortion of perception and judgement influence us, is described by e.g. HOBMAIR (1997):

- We do not see the behaviour but immediately interpret characteristics. Example: Otto is bobbing his legs up and down – meaning Otto is nervous.

- Improper generalisation: "You always have to interrupt me!"

- Selective perception – we only see what fits our 'knowledge'. Example: If a teacher thinks one student is very intelligent from initial information or the phenomenon of an initial impression, he inclines to regard statements from this pupil as very intelligent and stupid remarks as a slip-up. (Pygmalion effect).

- We do not see individuals but an actor. Examples: teachers, students, civil servants, West Germans, homeless persons, men and women, Germans and foreigners. With it we rather notice the 'typical', e.g. "the typical Japanese tourist has …", "civil servants are …".

- Similarity creates sympathy and closeness, a contrast position creates distance. A (un)sympathetic initial impression is overrated and distorts the processing of any information.

- Projective perception – we see what we wish to see. Example: a quarrel between children: "My son is well-behaved, the other one started the quarrel."

- Due to all our needs and desires, experiences, feelings and memories we look at the world through a subjective 'pair of glasses', let it be a chocolate bar or the half full or half empty glass.

We are often not aware of these and also other distortions in perception of persons and groups. We think that the reality is exactly as we see it. But in each phase these distortions play an important role that should not be underestimated, avoiding them will increase your competence.

… and now you!
Test these questions on yourself first. Begin a chat with yourself and write down answers to 1A (my topic) and 1B (my topic that I will work on throughout the whole book in reality) and 1C (1-2 concrete situations) as keywords into the field hereunder!

The questions in Chapters 3 to 6 will help to sharpen your view of the situations.

CASE EXAMPLE 1C ff.

Mr. Smith: "He darted into my office yesterday and said: Please get the documents for customer B ready quickly. I need them in one hour including the relevant calculations. Just imagine, one hour! As if I had nothing to do!"

As listener you now support the description of experienced situations with a non-verbal acknowledgement.

II. 2. NONVERBAL CONFIRMATION

2A Keep eye contact!
2B Smile and acknowledge what was said by nodding!
2C Take an equal or complementary posture to your partner!

Among the many possibilities to send out body signals, these three have been chosen, as they will have a strong influence on your partner and the relationship between the two of you. Through an intensive eye contact you signal interest and attention. Try an experiment next time you have a normal chat with someone – leave out the above listed non-verbal acknowledgement.

∼

2A Keep eye contact!

Avoid eye contact during the conversation! Look anywhere but not into his/her eyes and pay attention to his/her reaction! After the conversation ask him/her if she noticed any difference, if anything was different today from other times.

∼

2B Smile and acknowledge what was said by nodding!

Look into his/her eyes, but try to leave out smiles and nodding; observe how this affects his/her volubility. You can also deliberately take a different posture to your partner and then an equal or complimentary one. Complimentary here means that you can complement one another. If e.g. one bends forward the other leans back. To take up a similar posture signals agreement and resemblance, which gives sympathies as is known. There again sympathy achieves trust and openness and these are the basic requirements for conversations by mutual consent, friendship, team atmosphere and a healthy working climate.

∼

2c Take an equal or complementary posture to your partner!

If someone sits properly in front of you, then sprawl in the armchair. If the opposite number sprawls in his/her chair sit straight up. Pay attention to the course of the conversation and whether the posture is adopted or not.

The ABC of non-verbal acknowledgement also counts for telephone calls. Instead of eye-contact and nodding a positive stimulus is used ('Hmm!', 'Hmmmm!', 'Hmmm Hmmm!'). It signals presence and approval.

A smile is still a useful tool to encourage the volubility of your opposite number, although you cannot see him/her. Indeed, it is true: you can really notice if the person on the other end smiles. And your partner also notices whether you smile or are feeling low. Practised telephone users can even hear if his/her partner is sitting or lying down.

You can achieve good progress in your ability to listen if you adopt one fundamental philosophy: We will never be experts for other people's lives! Therefore, it is not advisable to transfer one's own interpretation and solutions as a 1:1 relation in form of advice into the other person's life. To ask for further details about a situation is more helpful than to suggest solutions, as additional keys to goals and ways to solutions are hidden herein, possibly not even known to your partner. You can establish the details in requesting your partner to outline the concrete situation as detailed and concrete as possible, from the beginning to the end.

During the following conversation you will have to lead your partner in such a way that you can vision the situation like a complete film and get to know the most important behaviour, conduct, thoughts, feelings and assessment of your opposite number.

II. 3. QUESTIONS TO BEHAVIOUR

3A What did you do? What did you say?
3B And then? What happened then?
3C What was the reaction? What did the other person say (do) then?

Psychology as a Science of behaviour and experience (HOBMAIR, 1997) distinguishes between the observable parts (behaviours) from the ones, that people can only observe on themselves (thoughts and feelings).

Everything you as the listener take in from descriptions of the situation, can be classified into one of the three categories behaviour, thoughts or feelings. Your own experiences will tell you if your partner left out one of those three categories. To leave out expected issues is very interesting, as many events are not left out per chance. In many cases this is a very important or awkward moment, i.e. the key to an important part of the solution. For modern behaviourist psychology these three categories to comprehend the human psyche via thoughts, feelings and behaviour are the royal way towards the comprehension of a problem.

Scientific results (GRAWE a.o., 1994) confirm the effectiveness of these proceedings in many areas. It is not necessary to delve into the past, as practised by the psychoanalysts ('soul analysis' founded by S. FREUD in the beginning of the 20th century) to find solutions for problems. The basic questions herein are useful to describe situations one experiences as a problem and also to find exceptions to these problems (see chapter 11).

3A What did you do? What did you say?

CASE EXAMPLE 3A

Coach: "So if I understood rightly, your superior entered your office and requested you to have the documents as well as the calculation ready in one hour. Is that right?"
Mr. Smith: "Yes, that's right."
Coach: "What did you reply?"
Mr. Smith: "One hour is really a short time."
Coach: "What did your superior reply?"
Mr. Smith: "He said something like: I will rely on you!"
Coach: "What did you do then?"
Mr. Smith: "Well, what could I do! I frowned and mumbled something like: Okay, we'll see!"

∽

3B And then? What happened then?

These easy-to-remember questions have an amazing variety of effects: You don't have to pay too much attention, you decrease your part of the speech, which will be greatly appreciated by your partner, and you can achieve a description of the situation in chronological sequence. This takes you to an almost complete description of the situation with less errors.

CASE EXAMPLE 3B

Coach: "And what happened then?"
Mr. Smith: "The boss left the office and I was really angry!"
Coach: "And then?"
Mr. Smith: "I cursed and then I called Kasulke, it's even worse for him, as the boss approaches him first most times!"

∽

3C What was the reaction? What did the other person say (do) then?

You can hardly help asking these questions, if you have not learned during the description of the situation what the other persons involved said or did. This question is necessary for the completion of the description of the situation and for the sensitization of your partner for the reaction of others.

CASE EXAMPLE 3C

Coach: "And what was the reaction of your superior, when you said: Ok we'll see."
Mr. Smith: "He nodded and was satisfied, he said 'Fine!' or words to that effect and then left!"
Coach: "And what happened then?"
Mr. Smith: "After my conversation with Kasulke I had to hurry up. Within a short time I made out transparencies, laid a folder out and compiled a rough calculation for two possibilities."
Coach: "And then?"
Mr. Smith: "I then went across and was ready prior to the customers arrival. The superior had a quick look at it, thanked me and that was it."

This case example shows clearly that Mr. Smith uses the same level of speech as the coach. His openness is also a sign that the relation between the two partners is fine and the coach's services are accepted. This is a very important basis for changes in behaviour later on.

The psychological school of behaviourism (*Psychological training of behaviour*, founded by WATSON 1913) is exclusively interested in the individual visible outward behaviour and his/her surroundings. The prime goal of the classic behavioural analysis is to understand how certain environmental stimuli can release certain reactions.

The ABC *of Behavioristic Psychology*:

A stands for *antecedent conditions,*
B stands for *behavioral response,* followed by
C *consequence.*

With behaviour-oriented questions almost every situation can be comprehended. They are also very helpful to complete incomplete statements. The following example and exercise gives you the opportunity to practice upon the technique. It is very important to question incomplete situations to get more information. It directs our attention to missing parts enabling us to purview our partner's situation from beginning to end with his/her eyes and feelings.

Examples to enquire after incomplete sentences:

Incomplete sentence	Enquiry
"That is difficult."	"What exactly is difficult?" "How does it show?"
"I feel worse."	"How does this show?" "How can you feel it?"
"I was angry!"	"On what? With whom?" "What did you do then?"

... and now you!
Get a more precise reality using questions. (solving page 137)

> He grumbles.
>
> Nothing nice is said.
>
> My frustration grows.
>
> I will not go along with that any more.

Did any 'Why' questions possibly slip in?
The disadvantage of these questions is that they divert from the current situation or are understood as reproach ("Why did you do something – stupid, naughty – like this?") Furthermore, behavioural sequences mostly happen unconsciously, such that an answer to this question would have to be reconstructed. Did no 'Why' questions slip in? My compliments to you!

It is not only very important to know about the visible behaviour but also to know the thoughts and feelings accompanying the behaviour. The conditions of feelings and emotion (e.g. moods from sad to cheerful), as well as situations of stress (e.g. from quiet to hectic) and needs (hunger, thirst, respect, security, confidence, desire) like our thoughts are always active.

According to DREES (1997) moods are the most important psychosomatic (relating to the interaction of psyche and body) factors of influence on the feeling of being alive, as you possess a pre-based strength. This encourages the selective perception and also has great influence on the description of past situations.

This can lead people to focus on the problem, get a negative outlook and remain in distress or – what would be more pleasant – if in a positive mood remain solution-oriented. Therefore it is very important to establish which thoughts and feelings accompany the behaviour.

II. 4. QUESTIONS TO THOUGHTS

4A What did you think at that moment?
4B Which thoughts made you say (do) that?
4C What did you feel?

You now know about any communication and actions and the next step is to determine the thoughts that arouse feelings and certain reactions. GARDNER (1989) assumes that the human being as a thinking being plans his actions, decides on one possibility and subsequently performs it.

Question 4C is deliberately kept open, so that your partner can mention thoughts as well as feelings, whichever concerns him/her.

CASE EXAMPLE 4ABC

Coach: "What went through your mind when your superior ordered this?"
Mr. Smith: "Impossible to get it done! He always comes out with these things at the last minute. He does that on purpose!"
Coach: "And what did you think when you said: Yes, I'll do it, although the time is short?"
Mr. Smith: "Let me think ... . I was already thinking about where I could find a similar calculation that I could use."
Coach: "But first you took your time and called Kasulke?"
Mr. Smith: "Yes, I had to let it out first, otherwise I wouldn't have been able to concentrate!"
Coach: "What did you feel during the telephone call?"
Mr. Smith: "I was very infuriated and in the end I was annoyed, but not so much any more."

The cognition is crucial to experience the situations, therefore I would like to give you the opportunity to note your thoughts ABC.

... and now you!
Recall the topic from 1B. Please think about a certain situation and fill in your thoughts in this situation in this box.

MEICHENBAUM (1977) proposed a procedure consisting of three phases to re-structure the thoughts:

The 1st phase consists of the realisation of the problematic thoughts and first of all facilitates a feeling of intensification in the control of the situation.

The 2nd phase meets the solution-oriented approach to determine new thoughts and behaviour to reach the goal. A concrete phrasing of the 2nd phase is e.g. SATIR's (1977)approach. According to this we can assume that there are rules for every statement.

These rules contain words like 'should', 'must', 'never', and 'always' connected to 'You should better ..., otherwise ... will happen!' For a child e.g. the worst threat is not to be loved or to be sent away. In this context rules change into an obligation; they have to be followed to survive or be loved. With her extremely positive concept of human nature, Satir predicts that one day humans will outgrow these inhuman rules due to the development of the five liberties.

The five LIBERTIES by Virginia Satir.

To see and hear what really is and not what should be.
To say what I think not what I should think.
To feel, what I really feel, not what I should feel.
To claim what I want without always waiting for permission.
To risk something without always covering myself first.

According to Satir (1995) restrictive rules are the basis of observable behaviour and a conversion of those into liberties is desirable for all situations which restrain us in everyday life. Therefore, Virginia Satir developed a method to converse such restrictive rules into conducive guidelines with the help of three steps. The basic principle is to dissolve the obligation of the rule and to see its message as an option.

Initial rule: *'I should not ask.'*
A background of this rule, e.g. the reason for a student will not enquire when he failed to understand something, could be the fear that everybody might think he is stupid, laugh at him and that the teacher would give him a bad assessment.

Step 1:
The 'should' or 'have to' is changed into 'can'. This will give the basis to extend the options.

"I can never ask."

Step 2:
A 'may not' or 'cannot' is changed into 'possibly can', a 'never' or 'always' into 'sometimes'.

"I can possibly ask questions."
"I can sometimes ask questions."

Step 3:
Now 'I can' is extended with three or more options, by inserting 'if …' to describe the accurate conditions.

"I can ask questions, if the lesson is with a certain teacher, if someone asked a question prior to me or if I want to check a train of thought."

> Liberty means responsibility.
> That is why most men dread it.
>
> GEORGE BERNHARD SHAW

Meichenbaum (1975) himself distinguishes various groups of thoughts, which e.g. help to cope with fears:

- Thoughts to prepare for a situation
  'I can and will devise a plan.'
  'I think more and better about my options to act. This is better than getting nervous.'
  No negative statements of oneself. Instead:
  'I will remain calm and think about a solution!'

- Confrontations
  Always step by step: 'I can handle this situation.'
  Relax and take a deep breath: 'Aaaahhh, good!'

- Coping
  'If the fear comes, just pause for a short while!'
  'Concentrate on what is set. What has to be done?'
  'That is not the worst that can happen!'
  'Just think about something else!'

- Self-acknowledgement
  'It worked, I made it.'
  'It wasn't as bad as I thought it would be.'
  'I'm happy about my progresses.'

In Phase 3 according to Meichenbaum people assess the consequences of their newly tested behaviour. This approach achieves new cognition incompatible to the former inhibiting ones. People notice the changes and get a new picture of themselves under the influence of the positive experiences. The solution-oriented approach offers a whole host of questions (note Chapter 10 : questions on scale), which will make the comparison easier.

It hasn't been unequivocally proven how thoughts and feelings interact. For instance we might like or dislike someone after having analysed the situation; therefore feelings would come after thoughts. Another view claims that feelings not necessarily derive from thoughts, but are subsequent reactions stimulated by the environment, e.g. we like or dislike someone spontaneously as ZAJONC (1980) established. Either way it is very important to find out about our partner's feelings.

II. 5. QUESTIONS ABOUT FEELINGS

5A Which feeling would best interpret your inner condition?
5B Was that your initial feeling in this moment?
5C What do you think the others involved felt?

The fast sequence in the observation of situations or persons, of ones own physiological changes (heart beat, tensions, perspiration, blushing etc) thoughts and feasibility of action within a situation influenced by social standardization leads to emotions and feelings.

The assessment of situations or feelings is different. The question: "How are you?" is mostly replied by a sorely practised reaction "Good". This is an assessment of feelings and does not say much about the intensity and quality of those feelings. But especially the naming and description of feelings is an important support for the personal development, because the clarity of feelings one has experienced is the basis for the positive feelings one strives for.

∼

5A Which feeling would best interpret your inner condition?

Especially for men it is difficult to put their feelings into words and to find the right words. Therefore it is important to request the naming of a feeling, insofar as the described feeling was actually the first or central feeling in this situation. As often hidden behind e.g. a feeling of rage is a feeling of fear or inferiority.

∼

5B Was that your initial feeling in this moment?

Imagine the situation of a mother waiting for her daughter in the evening. The daughter intended to be home about midnight, it is now half past and the mother cannot lie still any more, but wanders to and fro in the living room worrying. What do you think is the mother's demeanour, when the daughter enters the flat? Often the relief turns fear into anger and the daughter will feel it; she will not feel the worry and fear. Their relationship will be tenser than if the mother had shown her worries and relief.

Therefore, it is important, to find the initial feeling, to be able to express it. At the same time the feelings of other involved persons will be noted in problematic situations, or judged afterwards.

5C What do you think the others involved felt?

The reply to this question enables to put oneself in somebody's position. With an interval of time retrospectively and without the acute surge of adrenaline this is often possible and fruitful. Through this change of role a distance to one's own position is engendered, followed by a critical reflection of actions and words.

Which words can be found to express feelings?

Rage, pain, apprehension, despair, disgust, repulsion, pity, sorrow, horror, listlessness, worry, fear, hate, jealousy on one side and pleasure, joy, delight, love on the other side.

… and now you!
Use the table hereunder to note your feelings looking back on the situation you have chosen.

My ABC of feelings:

[ ]

Please pay attention if prior to an aggressive feeling is maybe a feeling of inferiority, helplessness or feeling small. This distinction is very important, because if one wants to leave the unwelcome condition, determine one's own goals and imagine the wonderful condition, where the problem is gone, it is a big difference, if you want to feel e.g. equal righted and esteemed or want to punch or kill someone full of revenge!

Case example 5ABC

Coach: "At the end or your telephone call with your colleague you were not as angry any more. The telephone call made an important difference to the initial condition, is that right?"
Mr. Smith: "Yes, that is right."
Coach: "Which feeling would best describe your inner condition, when the work was finished and you started to walk over to your superior?"
Mr. Smith: "Let me think, I was excited and a lot of thoughts went through my head. Of course I wanted that he accepted it and I was also still angry that he had surprised me."
Coach: "Was there perhaps another feeling prior to the anger?"
Mr. Smith: "Well yes, I was a bit frightened, he would be able to see the dislike on my face!"
Coach: "Ah yes, okay. And then you handed your work in. Do you know what your superior thought or felt?"
Mr. Smith: "Well, he seemed to be relieved and was obviously happy that I'd managed it and that we wouldn't meet the customer empty-handed."
Coach: "And how did you feel when you left his office?"
Mr. Smith: "I was satisfied with my work and had a cup of coffee first."
Coach: "And how did you feel about what your superior said?"
Mr. Smith: "A burden fell off my shoulders and, yes, I felt slightly happy."

Questioning demeanour, thoughts and feelings gives us a person's point of view. However, there are other sources, which, although you were not personally present during the conversation, can give information about the current situation and the persons present. This source is very useful for the discussion of the problem, but especially for the discussion about the solution! These questions are referred to as 'circular questions'.

II. 6. CIRCULAR QUESTIONS – QUESTIONS INTO THE VIEW OF OTHER IMPORTANT PEOPLE

6A What would your dearest relation say, if he/she was present here and now?
6B Have you spoken to someone else about this situation?
6C Assume we would ask XY, how would he/she notice that nothing/something has changed about your problem?

Instead of asking someone straight for his/her demeanour, abilities and reserves (raising of a self-portrait), circular questions take a different route. The client is asked to describe how other persons look at him (i.e. the assumed point of view by others) or what he/she believes how others see him/her.

Who are your most important relations?
Have you got a pet? What is it/are they called?
Do any influential persons from your past exist?
Which star would you have liked to be?

... and now you!
Please fill in the names of your circular partners whose opinion you set a high value on.

Contrary to comprehending the point of view by others, where a person is directly asked, the assumed point of view by others reflects how someone thinks others would describe him/her. These indirect important relations or persons involved in the situation are involved in the conversation although they are not really present.

Within systems and interactions it is very important to comprehend the reactions of every person involved in a problem, although they might not be present during the conversation or have been present during the described situation. People tend to adapt themselves to the picture which other partners may have about them in the sense of a self-fulfilling prophecy. On questioning the point of view of good friends or relations positive factors can be established, which will be helpful in solving the problem.

∼

6A What would your dearest relation say, if he/she was present here and now?

The questions about demeanour, thoughts and feelings give us a point of view about somebody. But there are further sources and even if you are not personally present during the conversation or during the relevant situation, they can give information regarding the current situation and persons present. This source is very helpful for the discussion about the problem, but especially for the discussion about the solution!

CASE EXAMPLE 6A

Coach: "Which persons or maybe also animals are or were important to you?
Mr. Smith: "Well, my wife, my daughter, my mother who is dead, my father, our dog Rex, my old form-master, those are the ones I can think of spontaneously."
Coach: "Is there also a star, singer, athlete or actor who you think is great?"
Mr. Smith: "Let me think, maybe the actor John Wayne."

Coach: "Okay, let's start with John Wayne. What would John Wayne say to your problem, if he were here?"

Mr. Smith: "(laughing) He would say: Get ready for the duel. Don't stand for that. Make a clean sweep."

Coach: "What would your father say to the account of your situation?"

Mr. Smith: "(thoughtful, earnest) He would say: Don't make such a fuss! That's what you get paid for, to follow your superior's instructions!"

Coach: "And your daughter?"

Mr. Smith: "She would say: Dad, don't get irritated again."

Coach: "And what would your wife think of?"

Mr. Smith: "She would say: Leave me alone, you know what I'm thinking!"

Coach: "And what does she think?"

Mr. Smith: "She says: Go and see your superior, tell what you want changed or look for another job!"

Coach: "Okay, what would your dog bark?"

Mr. Smith: "(smiling) He would say: Let your leash go and don't always be so careful!"

Coach: "So, if I understood this rightly, everyone except your father would say: Change your situation. Is that right?"

Mr. Smith: "Apparently so!"

With the help of these replies additional points of view are opened, where the partner changes into a new role with the exact knowledge of the situation and the involved persons. The replies open the possibility of self-reflection: 'What do I think, how my relations see me?'

... and now you!
What would your relations say now? Write down the point of view of important relations, let it be persons, animals, partners from the past or the star within yourself!

Even better would be to know instead of to assume. It is therefore important to find out if our partner can recall an actual reaction.

∼

6B Have you spoken to someone else about this situation?

Replies to this question reveal if there are any friends or other persons your client can speak with to his helpful satisfaction and whatever this help is. This reveals another point of view for the listener. The assumed point of view ('What do I assume how other people see me?') is a very important factor in a self-description, as via this distance to oneself, a lot of people find it easier to describe their strength and weaknesses.

CASE EXAMPLE 6B

> Coach: "You spoke to your colleague Kasulke. What did Kasulke say?"
> Mr. Smith: "He said, he was in an even worse situation, I should be happy!"

∾

> 6c Assume we would ask XY, how would he/she notice that nothing/something has changed about your problem?

The aim of this question is to get an insight into existing interaction of any points of view and to develop possible solutions from this perspective.

Question 6c can be chosen if no information is forthcoming from the questions 6A and 6B. Also it is a solution-oriented question the use of which is acknowledged by SCHMIDT (1995, in: S. DE SHAZER). He emphasises the importance of circular questions in the solution-oriented dialogue form he practices especially for the German culture: "Clients often foster the fantasy that someone would reproach them after a quick change, saying they could have stopped the symptoms much earlier, as it now seems to be relatively easy and quick to change. Therefore, it was well-tried for me to use a solution-oriented concept in the German culture working strictly solution-oriented on one side but using a lot of relation-oriented hypothetical circular questions, admittedly to clarify the meaning and effect it would have in the relationship as now resources are used and a quick success would occur."

CASE EXAMPLE 6C

> Coach: "How would e.g. Mr Kasulke notice that your relationship with your superior has changed to the better?"
> Mr. Smith: "Well I wouldn't moan as much, would be in a better mood. Maybe I wouldn't phone Kasulke as often."

The side effect of circular questions is to distance oneself from the problem, which can be looked upon as a preliminary step over to the solution orientation.

∾

II. 7. DISSOCIATION

7A Can you remember if there was anything pleasant or funny in this situation or relationship?
7B Please relate something nice, pleasant, that you have experienced, like e.g. about a nice person, your most favourite holiday place, animal, music, book or anything you can think of!
7C How did you manage to cope?

If you have established the problem mood your client is in and want to help him to change into a smiling-distanced mood, it would be useful to use the method of de-focussing (DREES, 1997). De-focussing means 'away from the focus'; a well-directed and used diversion of a problem-focused condition. Maybe you even know this method in everyday life as parents, e.g. if your child fell down and was hurt. You can ask the child to explain how the accident happened ("How did that happen?") A distance from the situation will help to focus on the facts, which will help to fade out the negative emotions.

∼

7A Can you remember if there was anything pleasant or funny in this situation or relationship?

Here you remain within the context of what your client is telling you. If your client goes into this question, his mood will automatically improve – the change into the solution-orientation is prepared.

CASE EXAMPLE 7A

Coach: "Has there ever been a situation where you and your superior had something to laugh about?"
Mr. Smith: "But there was …, on the Christmas do, exactly (smiling), that was funny, we did a play from the firm. Only short, but the rehearsals were also alright."

If this question does not enable a change, it would be an advantage to have a break. Changing rooms, offering something to drink or anything else, sometimes associates a change of mood and this might ease a lead-in for the client to leave the problem mood.

∼

7B Please relate something nice, pleasant, that you have experienced, like e.g. about a nice person, your most favourite holiday place, animal, music, book or anything you can think of!

Here it is necessary to link to previously heard information. If you are within your client's rooms, you can use pictures, furniture etc to put a question. Do not amplify the pleasant day of your client with gestures and facial expressions but use verbal compliments (see Chapter 13). You will generate a positive prevailing mood for the transition into the solution-orientation quicker this way.

CASE EXAMPLE 7B

Coach: "You performed in a play? But that is innovative.
Please tell me about it."
Mr. Smith: "It was as follows: We then had …"

The distinction between the person and his/her problem is important to further the distance of the problem mood and recover a relaxed condition. A lot of people unconsciously think that they themselves are the problem. But only a small part of their personality is blocked by the problem. Therefore it is important to distance oneself and to recover a point of view in which one's talent as expert on solving a problem moves into focal point. To get a first smile of your partner you can enter questions to how he/she managed something during this phase of the discussion.

∼

7c How did you manage to cope?

Questions to how somebody managed something, let him/her realise the talents that were encouraged by solutions to difficult situations in the past. By emphasising this it is possible to draw the attention to hidden talents or strategies, with which an uplift or a solution of the problem was reached. If you ask your partner where he found the strength to endure everything, you will learn about resources, which you can then usefully bring into the discussion. If a relapse had to be overcome, then e.g. the question: "How did you manage to overcome this relapse?" with an appropriate real and admiring undertone, the attention can be lead onto the time after the relapse and relevant solution-strategies accordingly.

CASE EXAMPLE 7C

Coach: "Can you tell me where you have got the strength to cope with this throughout all those years?"
Mr. Smith: "Well, yeah, it has been like this for some years. Hmm, for once of course my family helps me. Here in the office I sometimes switch on my radio and listen to classic music, the I can forget the worries, relax and concentrate on my work."

II. 8. TRANSITION TO SOLUTION ORIENTATION

8A   Is there another situation (another topic) you want to talk about?
8B   What we just talked about, ... do you really wish to change something about it?
8C   What are you prepared to do to solve your problems?

The goal of this part of the conversation is the transition or leap out of the problem mood into the solution orientation. If the previously described situation is clear and comprehensible for you, you can ask for any further situations regarding this topic. It is up to your partner whether he wants to add one or more situations or start a new topic. Now notes are necessary to avoid a confusion of the various situations.

∼

8A   Is there another situation (another topic) you want to talk about?

Herewith you ensure that your partner can 'enlighten his soul of' all encumbering feelings. This will heighten the probability for his transfer into solution-orientation.

CASE EXAMPLE 8A

> Coach: "I think I now know about your situation. Is there another situation or topic that you wish to discuss or shall we carry on working on this topic?"
> Mr. Smith: "Oh, I could tell you more about my superior. But let's work on this one closely!"

Questions to past topics can be illustrated in the following flow chart:

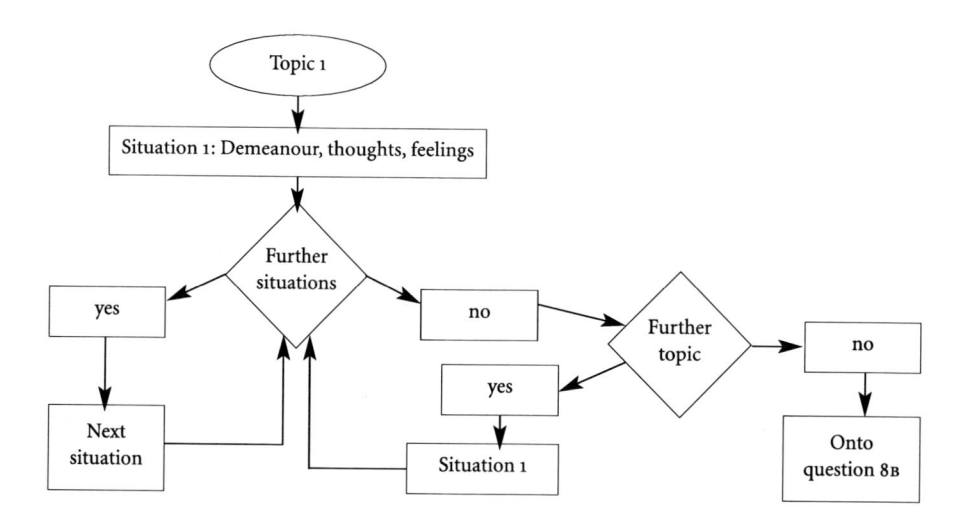

```
                    ┌─────────┐
                    │ Topic 1 │
                    └────┬────┘
                         ▼
        ┌────────────────────────────────────┐
        │ Situation 1: Demeanour, thoughts, feelings │
        └────────────────┬───────────────────┘
                         ▼
                    ◇ Further ◇
                    ◇ situations ◇
            yes  ╱      │       ╲  no      ◇ Further ◇     no
         ┌──────┐       │        ─────────▶◇  topic  ◇────────┐
         │      │       ▼                  ◇         ◇        │
         │      │      yes                       ▲            │
         ▼      │       │                        │            ▼
    ┌─────────┐ │       ▼                        │      ┌──────────┐
    │  Next   │ │  ┌──────────┐                  │      │   Onto   │
    │situation│─┘  │Situation 1│──────────────────┘      │question 8B│
    └─────────┘    └──────────┘                          └──────────┘
```

The mood one is in after a problem discussion might make a transition into solution orientation more difficult. You'll recognise this from a sad facial expression, being in low spirits and thoughts, which tend towards catastrophes ('Everything will end bad. I will never manage that') or self-reproaches ('I'm too stupid. I just can't do it and I'll never learn. Everything is my fault').

If you notice that your client's mood has lifted, now is a good time to ask the central question for the transition into the world of solutions.

∼

8B What we just talked about, … do you really wish to change something about it?

The following 'Yes, I want to …' is a self-confession and means to accept responsibility for the change and the necessary steps. This includes not to make others responsible for one's own problems, but to recognise that it is in one's own power to find solutions and tackle them.

The 'Yes, I do want to …' is an important signal to set off, it should be said convincingly and with a strong voice. Facial expression, posture and voice have to be conforming to be believable, such that the set off will be more than just a lip-service!

CASE EXAMPLE 8B

Coach: "Do you wish to improve your relation with your superior and are you prepared to do your part?"
Mr. Smith: "Yes, by all means!"

MEHLMANN & RÖSE wrote (1999):
"We don't dare because the solution would be difficult, but as long as we don't dare it seems to stay difficult."

> *No-one will know one's own strength until he/she's tested it.*
>
> J.W. VON GOETHE

The feeling of minority that we have prior to difficult and embarrassing situations, is changed into a feeling of superiority step by step; we experience ourselves able to act powerful and free to cross our own barriers – obstacles which mostly are put in the way by ourselves.

~

8C What are you prepared to do to solve your problems?

The question to what one is prepared to sacrifice to get rid of a problem, is an important indication for the emotional importance of the problem and its disappearance. Additionally, initial strategies are already mentioned here which will ease the transition into solution-orientation.

CASE EXAMPLE 8C

Coach: "What are you willing to do, to overcome your problems?"
Mr. Smith: "Well, try a new route and do some things differently!"

... and now you!
Do you want to change something and are you also prepared to do your part? Write down in your words your willingness to change parts of your behaviour and thinking to enable yourself reaching your goal less difficult and easier.

And finally:
To enable you to look at the contents of the problem-discussion at any time, you will receive a survey showing the essential questions. With this frame of 24 questions and tipes that you can adopt to your personal style, you will create an extremely clear and comprehensible discussion structre, which will encourage the flow of communication and at the same time creates an impartant assumption for the transfer into solution-orientation.

∽

Checklist for problem discussion

1. Invitation to discuss a problem
   1A What is on your mind? What concerns you?
   1B What would you like to begin with?
   1C Please outline a concrete situation?

2. Non-verbal acknowledgement
   2A Keep eye contact!
   2B Smile and confirm what was said by nodding!
   2C Take an equal or complementary posture to your partner!

3. Questions about behaviour
   3A What did you do? What did you say?
   3B And then? What happened then?
   3C What was the reaction? What did the other person say (do) then?

4. Questions about thoughts
   4A What did you think at that moment?
   4B Which thoughts made you say (do) that?
   4C What did you feel?

5. Questions about emotions
   5A Which feeling would best interpret your inner condition?
   5B Was that your initial feeling in this moment?
   5C What do you think the others involved felt?

6. Circular questions – Enquiry about the view of important people
   6A What would your dearest relation say, if he/she was present here and now?
   6B Have you spoken to someone else about this situation?
   6C Assume we would ask XY, how would he/she notice that nothing/something has changed about your problem?

7. Dissociation
   7A Can you remember if there was anything pleasant or funny in this situation or relationship?
   7B Please relate something nice, pleasant, that you have experienced, like e.g. about a nice person, you most favourite holiday place, animal, music, book or anything you can think of!
   7C How did you manage to cope?

8. Transition to solution-orientation
   8A Is there another situation (another topic) you want to talk about?
   8B What we just talked about, … do you really wish to change something about it?
   8C What are you prepared to do to solve your problems?

III. INTRODUCTORY WORDS TO DISCUSS A SOLUTION

The principle of solution orientation is based on the concept of self-efficacy as a central element of the social and educational theory (BANDURA, 1986). Self-efficacy is the belief to be able to successfully cope with a certain situation, the feeling for ones own abilities. Self-efficacy as belief in oneself affects the perception on situations, the motivation and achievement.

If we do not feel up to meet the demands, we tend to avoid any such situation, even if we have the ability to successfully manage it. We do not act or do not finish an action, because we believe that we have not got the necessary abilities. But if the positive feeling of self-efficacy appears we will confront the situation, achieve success in most cases and are also able to apply our abilities to new situations.

> *Without enthusiasm the strongest vigour of our mind will sleep. There is a tinder within ourselves that wants to spark.*
>
> J. G. VON HERDER

The feeling of self-efficacy not only influences which situations, activities or strategies we will choose in every day life, but also how much persistence and energy we will use. ZIMBARDO (1992, page 423) describes the following mechanism: "The expectation for success or failure is changeable, depending on the responses to achievements. However, it is more likely that the expectation of self-efficacy produces the response and such turns into fulfilling prophecies."

In other words: if we or other people see our own ability, we will begin to do the right things (effectiveness) and to do things right (efficiency). With enough self-confidence we will address the challenging situation and the prophecy will actually be fulfilled.

If you solve problems according to the causal principle, you first have to work on the cause of the problems in the past, analyse problems, complain about deficiencies and find diagnostic categories (depressed, addicted, ill, be in a bad way).

Upon comprehension of the concrete situation the solution-oriented communication subsequently begins to work out and shape solutions.

> Do not make the pain unbearable with endless moaning!
>
> SOPHOKLES

Solutions are not only mentioned as goals, but the aim is to experience the solutions of the problems, i.e. the imaginary anticipation of e.g. a certain situation or a full day without the problem and without the unpleasant feelings it produces.

If you manage to create a 'preceding optimism' an enormous energy for the change will emerge. This energy fights the internal blockades and our internal comprehension of problems and their solutions. In the epilogue GUNTHER SCHMIDT (1995, in: S. DE SHAZER, pages 236/237) described his experience with German clients compared to American clients: "In our culture the need for history, senses etc and also the search for causes seems to be even bigger. Especially, if a long term problem is being treated, over here I experience more often that the person concerned cannot believe that something could be changed in a few meetings, yes, they also suspect that the severity of their suffering is just not being appreciated any more."

If you decide to think and act solution-oriented, then four fundamental assumptions are of great importance:

A Solutions and Problems are two totally different things.

Our mind often functions via associations i.e. on top of problems we always think of further problems. One problem story revives the next one. On top of things that do not work out everything else that does not function is also added. Thus a vicious circle of problem mood and moaning is initiated, which wwill not change anything. To be able to break through this vicious circle it is important to leave the problem mood e.g. via disassociation and to use visions of the solution to move towards dealing with a solution.

Let's look at a case where a woman regards her problem to be the lack of courage to stand up for her beliefs. Now all the situations lacking courage could be picked out as a central theme in every conversation. During her recounting the partner will also activate the memorised emotions. The accumulation of unpleasantly experienced failures rather ensues a paralysing atmosphere. Speaking about problems is the main emphasis of the conversation.

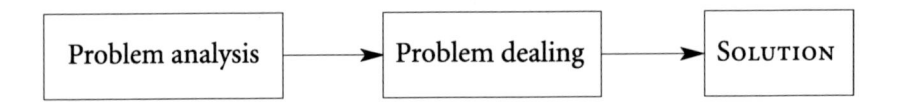

```
┌──────────────────┐     ┌──────────────────┐     ┌──────────────┐
│ Problem analysis │ ──▶ │ Problem dealing  │ ──▶ │   SOLUTION   │
└──────────────────┘     └──────────────────┘     └──────────────┘
```

But it is much more pleasant to search for courage in the past and to talk about successful situations, where courage lead to a good mood and self-confidence.

In the area of therapy MILTON H. ERICKSON (1954) published the crystal-ball-technique. He put people under hypnosis into a more successful future. Then he suggested that they move from the successful future into their past. De Shazer found out that the use of this technique gets people to change their conduct. The pleasant changes to achieve a solution as experienced in thought and feelings, will change the perception of problem focussing into an optimistic solution-orientation.

```
┌─────────────────┐      ┌─────────────────┐      ┌───────────┐
│ Visioned solution│ ───► │ Solution dealing│ ───► │ SOLUTION  │
└─────────────────┘      └─────────────────┘      └───────────┘
```

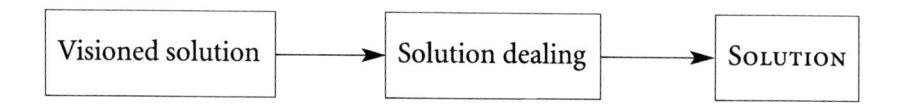

Talking about the successful coping in difficult situations in the past will achieve an optimistic solution mood. This will result to perceive the possible solution to a problem as less difficult or easier, as it has already worked out in the past. This manner contradicts the fundamental assumption especially in Germany that problems and their causes have to be cleared before concentrating on the solutions.

If you e.g. live in Hamburg but do not like it there any more, problem focussing or analytically oriented people would try to find out why they don't like to live in Hamburg any more for months and years. Instead it seems more sensible to look for a more pleasing alternative. The chosen place would appear as an attractive goal and would expedite the change!

Worse than difficulties is the tendency to avoid them.

OESCH

B Problem-focussing people block themselves.

If people pay more attention to the problems and moan over conditions, instead of changing them, they are focussing on the problems. This would lead to a repetition of the affairs, which are associated with unpleasant feelings and failures; a waste of time and energy!

Feeling sorry for oneself is the worst service for oneself

OESCH

Problem-focussing people are often unable to see that they are not only responsible but also hold the ability to change their conditions in life. Instead they look for the responsibility in their surroundings: the partner, the superior, the government, the others are guilty or should change something: "It is not my fault that my superior is like that." Such thoughts do lift the self-efficacy for a short while as the responsibility for unpopular situations is shifted away from themselves onto the environment. However, this would not change a lot about the actual facts, indeed they are even reinforced, as no action is taken.

Heaven never helps those who won't act.
SOPHOKLES

For Christopher Reeves – once superman, now confined to a wheelchair – a hero is an ordinary person, who finds the strength to find his/her way with persistence in a seemingly hopeless situation. Everybody bears in him/herself the possibility to live an heroic life!

> C Solution-oriented people use problems as an opportunity to get active – they feel optimistic in advance.

Are you a person full of vitality, who looks upon problems as a challenge or can you carry away other people? Have you got a high value on the scale for solution-orientation?

Or, in other words: What was it like last time you carried someone away or got carried away yourself? Can you recall such a situation? Make yourself aware of this picture once more. If you remember it vividly, you will know that you have the capability to carry others away. You therefore only have to activate your internal solution-orientation. The 'how' is described in the next Chapters.

One's life span remains the same, whether on laughs or cries throughout.

FROM JAPAN

If your answer to a question about using your capabilities is: 'I cannot!', the solution will be within the demand you are requested to put on yourself: 'If I want to achieve something I have never achieved, then I will have to do something I have never done before!'

D   The solution is known!

It is always interesting to observe that in 99% of all cases the solution is known. Only in a few cases a non-existing knowledge causes problem-focussing. It is instead the non-existing willingness or lacking courage to tackle changes that are obstructing solution-orientation or the solution itself. Lacking willingness is mainly based on internal rules. You have already experienced how to change them. Sometimes it is based on a certain idleness, but with the picture of a future free of problems this idleness can mostly be overcome, whilst it radiates an attractive effect and a seemingly magnetic one.

How can you increase your activity?
There are some good reasons to stick to well-known and well-tried methods. As no-one can say for sure if an experience in the future would be more satisfactory for one's own needs. Tackle the situation with optimism and you will experience the change as a pleasant possibility to achieve a success. Also your positive charisma will grow.

American scientists like DE SHAZER, WEAKLAND and others have used solution-oriented procedures in the area of short-time family therapy and managed to decrease the average therapy duration of families from 30 hours to under 4 hours, whereby the therapy success is measured after two years and was above 60% of all persons questioned (and thus as high as with a long-time therapy). This means, it works out!

And whenever something works out, Rule 1 counts.

If something works out, make more of it!

Exercise for Rule 1 for you:

- What is going well at the moment? Please note the topic, that comes to your mind to this question.
- What have you done for it, what is your engagement, the warranty for success?
- To which topic where you encounter problems can you transfer this engagement?

Topic:

Success warranties, my engagement:

New topics, where I can transfer the engagement to:

You have known this rule for years, as like the German psychologist HEIDER (1958) described, 'normal, average' people have their own theories on solution, to which they will listen. Of course this also creates a 'superstitious attitude' i.e. behaviour that accidentally met with a successful attitude, is taken as a lucky charm for the future. I know someone who has been running to the toilet during an important football game of his team for decades, as in the past his team had shot two goals during this time. Of course it does not help, but the behaviour, as irrational as it sounds, is deeply rooted and the tradition is continued.

Imagine you have been suffering from a rash to your feet for three months now. If, as solution-oriented person, you suspect your new pair of shoes or new pair of socks you would not wear them any more. If you think that the rash is from a visit to a swimming pool, you would avoid the place or wear flip-flops.

You use Rule 2:

If something doesn't work out, do something else!

If a new behaviour proves to be effective, in that it ends the experienced problem and the suffering, it is kept according to Rule 1. As problem-focussing person you would not do anything like it, but you would moan about the itch and a subject of your conversations would be what has not helped so far.

Exercises for Rule 2 for you:

- What is bothering you at the moment?
  Please note the problem or difficulty.
- What have you done so far?
- What will you do differently from now on?

Problem:	
Done so far:	New from now on:

It is often sufficient to recall strategies that have led to success once. To get clarity on what would be the best solution for our partner, it is best to ask him/her what he/she would do different or what would happen, after they got rid of the problem. The above example illustrates Heider's and also the solution-oriented point of view that no scientific-psychological theory to predict your behaviour is as useful as your own. Your belief about the causes as well as your belief about solutions and goals will determine your actions. But how? Do make this experience for yourself, the wonderful experience that starts with a wonderful question!

III. 9. QUESTIONS TO GOALS AND FUTURE

9A The miracle question
9B The 'as if'-question
9C What precisely are your professional/private goals?
    The table of decision

The imagination of a problem-free future will motivate successful action. The best known technique to produce this vision is the miracle question. Read it out loud and let it have an effect on you.

9A The miracle question

When you retire to bed tonight, a fairy will come with her magic stick and everything we spoke about, every problem has found a solution. As you were asleep you will not know that the miracle has happened! So as you wake up tomorrow morning ...

... how will you initially notice that the miracle has happened?
... what is different than normally?
... who else would notice? And how?
... and now you!

Write down your miracle and its shaping here and now!

> How will I notice the miracle?
>
> What will be different than normally?
>
> How will the others notice?

This question not only includes the understanding of the point of view but also the circular understanding of other persons' points of view. A question to you, dear reader: Has anything changed on yourself? Maybe your posture, breathing or facial expression? Your replies to the miracle question awake the expectancy of a positive change (DE SHAZER, 1995) and the attached pleasant sides of a successful experience.

One pleasure banishes a hundred worries.

FROM JAPAN

Feel the pleasant strength and experience the change of your perception: A half-empty glass turns into a half-full glass and the imagination to be able to live through frightening situations in absolute command revives a feeling of inner contentment. Not only the 'away from the problem' but definitely the 'up to a pleasant goal' is eminently motivating.

CASE EXAMPLE 9A

Coach: "Mr. Smith, I would like to put an unusual question to you: When you retire to bed tonight, please imagine that a miracle will occur during the night. We both know that miracles don't exist, but we can imagine them for a moment, can't we. Well, the miracle happens over night and the problem with your superior, Mr. Smith, has vanished! But because you were asleep you won't know that the miracle has happened. So if you enter the office tomorrow morning, how will you initially notice that the miracle has happened? What will be different?"

Mr. Smith: "Well," (leaning back, clasping his hands behind his head and smiling) "then the boss would come in and shake my hand. He will have his door open and I can see him to co-ordinate the day planning. We might have lunch together some time. And if I've worked well he'll show his appreciation."

Coach: "How will he do that?"

Mr. Smith: "Maybe he'll tell me, maybe even during a meeting with all the colleagues: Mr. Smith that was nice work."

Coach: "And how would you feel?"
Mr. Smith: "(beaming) Well, splendid."
Coach: "And how would your wife notice?"
Mr. Smith: "Well, I would tell her. Maybe with a glass of red wine. Or we'll just go into town again to our favourite Italian restaurant. We haven't been there for a long time!"

If you want to build a ship, do not start collecting wood, cutting planks or delegating labour, but arouse men's yearning for the ocean.

By Antoine de Saint-Exupery

A second possibility to phrase a goal is to ask an 'as if'-question, that also allows to live through the image of a pleasant future.

9B The 'as if'-question

Assume we would meet again in a year and discuss this topic and how you managed to gain control, …

… what will you tell me?
… how will you notice that you have managed to gain control?
… who else will have noticed and how?
… what will be different?

"Assume the problem … would be sorted. How would you know?"
"Assume you'd have to change something tomorrow … How would you begin?"

This unusual verbal technique of the future tense assumes that you are able to put yourself in a condition where the problem has been successfully solved by means of an imagined journey.

Imagine that you have solved your problems in an outstanding supremely well manner. You have therefore been invited to a reputable talk show to tell about it. What will you tell?

The basic acceptance that a problem has vanished opens a pleasant distance to the problem. Distance to the problem is important, to be able to come out of the problem-focussing and oppressing feelings.

The interest of a solution-oriented partner turns away from the topic 'problems and their causes' to the topic 'solutions and how they function'. Therefore it is a useful experience to use time intervals as a method to disassociate one-self from the problems. This can bring you into the future or into dreams about the past.

CASE EXAMPLE 9B

Coach: "Mr. Smith, assume we'd meet again in a year and talk about this topic and how you managed to sort it out. What would you tell me?"
Mr. Smith: "Well, I would be able to tell you that I had a good conversation with my superior. And that he then changed something, such that my dream came true!"
Coach: "Assuming you'd have to change something tomorrow with what would you begin?"
Mr. Smith: "I'd get an appointment."

The difficulty to leave problem-focussing is described by Paulo Cuelho (*The Alchimist,* page 28):

"It is what you have always wanted to do. Every youth knows what their destiny in life is. Everything is so easy in this phase of life and they are not afraid to imagine everything and to wish for what they would like to do in their life. However, whilst time goes by, a mysterious force tries to convince us that it is impossible to realise our personal journey through life."

Vision production can and has to take unusual routes:
'What will be in the papers about you in 2010?' This form of vision production also helps you to produce clarity and attraction to your goals.

"Imagine you would have the task to write a novel about your life and to bring it to a 'happy end'. You start with the presence and all your problems. What will you write, how will you have managed to lead your life to success?"

There are as many creative ideas for visions as there are people who think about their dreams. Visions are important as we can derive goals from them, long as well as short term goals. One could also say:

Goals are visions with a closing date!

Only if you are clear about your goals, you can consciously use your energies, power and resources to reach your goals. If you have no idea how this wonderful situation will be or would be if the problem had been sorted out, then a task (Chapter 17) would help to fill this gap and to increase the motivation for change.

> People can be divided in three classes: the inflexible ones, the flexible ones and the ones who move.
>
> From Arabia

As finding your goal is of immense importance for your future, please take a lot of time for yourself and your system (family, work group) and bring clarity into your mutual and individual goals.

~

9C What precisely are your professional/private goals?

Here you can make a list of a 1- or 5-year plan. List your goals and enquire if they will fulfil the following cirteria (by HENNIG & EHINGER, 1998):

a clear, precise description	*I want to get worked up less ... how do you want to react instead?*
a positive formulation	*what would you like to do most?*
meaningful	*what is important about it?*
form partial goals	*I should read more ... how many hours a day would you like to read?*
describe the first step	*which book? until when?*
evaluate the realisation	*is that possible?*

If your goals and the vivid ideas are not contrary to the successful achievement, then you can begin the change on the behavioural level.

But what if I can choose between two alternatives and I have not yet seen a clear picture of the wonderful situation in my mind? In most cases an assessment of the alternatives presents itself, making it possible to break through the constant brooding by writing down the pros and contras of the arguments as well as their assessment and to expedite the decision progress for a goal or a way.

A person without a plan is like a ship without steering.

OESCH

To compile a decision-table:

1. Name your alternatives and write them down.
2. Write down the advantages and disadvantages. Distinguish between short- and long-term arguments.

After the rational collection of arguments two decision supporting steps in form of questions can be attached:

3. Which spontaneous thought came up whilst reading through your short-term advantages in A (please write this down!) Please complete the draft for long-term and other advantages and disadvantages.
4. Which feeling comes up if you read the thought and arguments (fear, confidence, doubt, joy)?
Complete this for all listed advantages and disadvantages.

The following decision-table explains the action in the topic to choose an occupation:

The decision-table – sample: choice of occupation

Alternative A	Alternative B	Alternative C
Study business management	training for IT-businessman	open a shop for mobile phones

Advantages | Advantages | Advantages

Short-term	short-term	short-term
Easy life	*Job for the future*	*independence*

Long-term	long-term	long-term
More money	*money*	*move*
Prestige	*independence*	

Thoughts about the advantages
Exciting	*interesting*	*well …*

Feelings about the advantages
Joy	*feels good*	*doubts*

Disadvantages | Disadvantages | Disadvantages

Short-term	short-term	short-term
Little money		*– high risk*
Study pressure		*debts*

Long-term	long-term	long-term
Unemployment	*little money*	*–*

Thoughts about the disadvantages
I can't treat myself for years	*that will be a hard time*	*no leave, 14 hours work a day – oh Lord*

Feelings about the disadvantages
unsure	*feel confident*	*too much*

If you now compare the thoughts and feelings, you will clearly feel the inner preference for alternative B. To check this, you can let your partner evaluate the found arguments (without thoughts and feelings).

5. Evaluate your arguments on a scale of 1 to 3,
   1 = less important, 2 = important, 3 = very important.

Auswertung der Entscheidungstafel – Beispielthema: Berufswahl

Alternative A	Alternative B	Alternative C
Study business management	training for IT-businessman	open a shop for mobile phones

Advantages

Alternative A		Alternative B		Alternative C	
Short-term		short-term		short-term	
Easy life	(3)	*Job for the future*	(2)	*independence*	(2)
Long-term		long-term		long-term	
More money	(3)	*money*	(3)	*move*	(2)
Prestige	(1)	*independence*	(2)		

∑ Advantages

A = 7 points   B = 7 points   C = 4 points

Thoughts about the advantages
Exciting   *interesting*   *well …*

Feelings about the advantages
Joy   *feels good*   *doubts*

Disadvantages

Alternative A		Alternative B		Alternative C	
Short-term		short-term		short-term	
Little money	(3)	–		*high risk*	(1)
Study pressure	(1)			*debts*	(3)
Long-term		long-term		long-term	
Unemployment	(3)	*little money*	(2)	–	

∑ Disadvantages

A = 7 points   B = 2 points   C = 4 points

Thoughts about the disadvantages
I can't treat myself for years   *that will be a hard time*   *no leave, 14 hours work a day– oh Lord*

Feelings about the disadvantages
unsure   *feel confident*   *too much*

6. Now add the assessed advantages of alternative A and the disadvantages of B and C, as this all speaks for A; do the same with alternatives B and C.

For A the advantages (7 points) and the disadvantages of B (2 points) and C (4 points) count –> 13 points;
For B the advantages (7 points) and the disadvantages of A (7 points) and C (4 points) count –> 18 points;
For C the advantages (4 points) and the disadvantages of B (2 points) and A (7 points) count –> 13 points.

In this example the decision problem is solved by the principle of the written word with the help of rational comprehensible steps. This empties the mind for the next steps, in this case for the vision of a successful application for a training for IT businessman.

Use the decision table on the next page for one of your current decisions! Please use the same sequence and state your thoughts and feelings before you assess the found arguments.

CASE EXAMPLE 9C

    Coach: "Mr. Smith, what exactly are your goals in a discussion with your superior?"
Mr. Smith: "Hmm, I would like for him to respect me. Yes, that he appreciates that I work for him! I don't know if he does!"

Your decision table - your topic:

Alternative A

Advantages
Short-term
( )
( )
Long-term
( )
( )

∑ Advantages
A = points

Thoughts about the advantages A

Feelings about the advantages A

Disadvantages
Short-term
( )
( )
Long-term
( )
( )

∑ Disadvantages
A = points

Thoughts about the disadvantages A

Feelings about the disadvantages A

Alternative B

Advantages
short-term
( )
( )
long-term
( )
( )

B = points

Thoughts about the advantages B

Feelings about the advantages B

Disadvantages
short-term
( )
( )
long-term
( )
( )

B = points

Thoughts about the disadvantages B

Feelings about the disadvantages B

Alternative C

Advantages
short-term
( )
( )
long-term
( )
( )

C = points

Thoughts about the advantages C

Feelings about the advantages C

Disadvantages
short-term
( )
( )
long-term
( )
( )

C = points

Thoughts about the disadvantages C

Feelings about the disadvantages C

III. 10. SCALE QUESTIONS

10A Scale of the present condition
10B Scale of confidence
10C Scale of the frequency of problem exceptions

The thorough comprehension of the present condition using behaviour-oriented questions can gain a lot from a solution-oriented approach of a scale question. Thus establishing the distance to the desired goal condition as well as the distance to the highest problem condition. The introduction of numerical scaling is a big help as it can be used for various cultures.

Furthermore, clients with an intuitive dislike to answering miracle questions or who love mathematical-technical tasks would find this way more acceptable.

The decimal scale was chosen, as it offers plenty of room for differences also in complex problems. The starting point lies in the positive area and not on 0, as this way the association of 0 = 'to be nothing' can be avoided. Furthermore, there are plenty of possibilities for distinction, such that the phenomenon of avoiding extremes (tendency for medium) is also accounted for.

Scale questions are a useful technique if you already know enough of your client's problems or if the way of the dialogue is solution-oriented in such a way that you can say: I do not need to know so much about the problem - not about the causes anyway; it is enough that I can work with my client within the positive world of solution. You can use scales for miscellaneous topics and in different phases of the conversation:

Transfer to solution-orientation

1. To scale the importance of a topic
2. To scale the confidence in a change
3. To scale the inner motivation

To set goals and partial goals

1. To scale the goal clarity
2. To scale the appropriateness of the steps
3. To scale the willingness of risk taking

To scale changes

1. To scale the frequency of problem exceptions (see Chapter 10c)
2. To scale the initial progress
3. To scale the effectiveness

The answer to the miracle question describes a goal condition that one wants to achieve. Several steps have to be taken for the fulfilment. These strategic steps determine exactly the difficulties in daily life and are the reason to remain in a present condition during problem-focussing. Scale questions are useful in many ways to find the starting point of the progress and changes towards a solution and at the same time not to bother with the description of the problem from the past.

10A Scale of the present condition

Please imagine a scale of 1-10, whereas 10 stands for the wonderful condition of the goal you just described. 1 stands for nothing happened. Where between 1 and 10 would you evaluate yourself today?

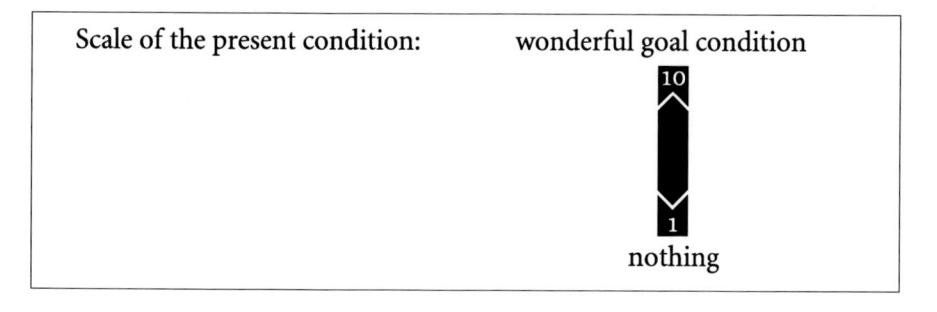

Scale of the present condition:	wonderful goal condition
	10 ↕ 1
	nothing

Case example 10a

>Coach: "Mr. Smith, please imagine a scale of 1-10, whereas 10 stands for the wonderful condition of the goal you just described. 1 stands for nothing happened. Where between 1 and 10 would you evaluate yourself today?"

Mr. Smith: "Between 3-4."

To successfully manage a partial goal the question after one's internal confidence to reach that partial goal is essential, as the inner motivation strongly varies with the subjectively felt attraction for the goal.

The 10-stone-exercise is one possibility to sense the present condition (BUCHNER, 1995). Your client receives 10 stones to take in his/her hand. If the confidence to reach his/her goal is 100%, he/she keeps 10 stones. In doubt he/she pushes 4 stones away, expressing a confidence of 60%.

∼

10b Scale of confidence

How confident do you feel about reaching your described goal? If you are totally sure, you'll keep all 10 stones. If you are totally unsure, you'll push all stones away, in between you can grade!

You can let your creativity run free: If there are 10 pens on your desk or 10 sweets or 10 nuts, these can also be used to sense the present condition on scale. A sketch of the scale also increases the attention and ability to memorise this part of the conversation. You can also determine the inner confidence of your client from his/her tone of voice: shaky or steady, unsure or precise, loud or quiet!

There are tools available in the Chapters 12 to 15 to assist you in increasing your client's confidence in his/her own thinking and acting with the use of various question techniques and the use of compliments. This form ofscaling is now well-known due to the behavioural methods of the systematic desensitising. After an analysis of the situation in a topic of fear (e.g. fear of heights) the client learns to relax before he/she declares a goal. The final goal is preceded by 10 achievement goals, chosen by the client and starting with the easiest partial goal. Step 1 can be the first step on a ladder, lingering and looking about for 3 minutes; step 2 to linger on the second step for 4 minutes and so on ....

It is no surprise that exactly this method has the highest grade of success of over 80% in fighting phobia (excessive fears).

CASE EXAMPLE 10B

> Coach: "Mr. Smith, how confident are you on a scale of 1-10 to lead this conversation? If for example we take the 10 sweets in your box. Keeping 10 sweets means absolute confidence, giving 10 sweets to me means: there will not be a conversation with all probability. How many sweets will you give me?"
>
> Mr. Smith: "2 at the maximum."

Although people tend to generalise unpleasant details ('I can never climb on anything', 'I always think I will feel sick and fall down') there are always successes to be shown ('of course I have already climbed trees. How often I did not fall down? I guess about 200 times!') It is therefore necessary to look upon successful exceptions of the problem, as such an awareness can assist in coping with actual conflicts.

10C Scale of the frequency of problem exceptions

How many exceptions of the problem, i.e. successful experiences, were there? Choose a mark on the scale between 10 (a lot of successes in the past) and 1 (only a few successes!

> Scale of successful experiences: a lot of successes
>
> How many exceptions of the problem
> were there onthis scale, reaching from
> a lot of to a few successes. You can grade
> in between.
>
> a few successes

Your partner does not have to enter figures into this scale form, a cross will be sufficient.

CASE EXAMPLE 10C

> Coach: "Mr. Smith, how many exceptions of the problem were there? Please put your cross on this scale, the top means: a lot of respectful attestation by your superior. The bottom means: no respectful attestation by your superior."
>
> Mr. Smith: "Well, I would say in the middle!"

After you've received a response from your partner, you can look at two periods:

1. into the past (see Chapters 11-12), as you ask for successful exceptions of the problem and the underlying talents,
2. into the future (see Chapter 13), involving the determination of the next step towards the goal considering ones own talents.

If your partner cannot recall anything at this time and evaluates the question for successes with 1, it could be a task (see Chapter 17) for him/her to recall such successes or better times for the next conversation (see Chapter 11-12).

Mehlmann & Röse (1999, page 25) explicitly indicate the importance of exceptions of any problems: "Exceptions prove the rule, that there almost always were and are trouble-free times. After all this means that our clients were able to cope at certain times and therefore also know how they can cope. Therefore, there are always already solutions!'

∽

These exceptions of the problem will be investigated in the following section.

III. 11. QUESTIONS ABOUT SUCCESSFUL EXCEPTIONS OF THE PROBLEM

11A When in the past has it been better?
11B Please describe a successful situation!
11C What is different in situations where the difficulty appeared less strong/was not there?

The trip to past successes will have several positive effects on your conversation: The unpleasant descriptions of a problem are removed by the pleasant solution account, such producing positive feelings. Thereafter you can talk about the skills that were available in the past and plan their 'recycling' for the current situation.

11A When in the past has it been better?

With this form of question it is assumed that there have been times when your partner felt better and that he/she achieved this him/herself. Questions about exceptions as well as questions with regards to goals and future solutions only should be asked after the problem has been sufficiently 'appreciated' (HENNIG/EHINGER, 1998).

CASE EXAMPLE 11A

Coach: "What worked at least now and then?"
Mr. Smith: "Well, if we did not expect any customers, the boss' door is open. And once a month we have a meeting."
Coach: "Can you recall a meeting where you felt your boss' respect?"
Mr. Smith: "Yes, once during a meeting, he really wanted to pull something through, which would not have met our target group. So I pointed out to him, that this would not meet the goals of our business."

11B Please describe a successful situation!

If you as listener ask questions to behaviour, thoughts, feelings and the point of view of other important persons, you will receive a better insight in successful situations and about your partner. Use the questions of Section 3-6 to let your partner re-live the intensive feeling of his/her success.

CASE EXAMPLE 11B

>Coach: "Please describe this situation! Can you recall this meeting, where you felt respected by your superior?"
>Mr. Smith: "Five of us were sat together and I told him to his face that this decision would not meet our goals."
>Coach: "How did the others react?"
>Mr. Smith: "They found this extremely courageous. One female colleague told me that she would not have dared to say this."
>Coach: "How did you feel then?"
>Mr. Smith: "That gave me a sense of satisfaction, I took a deep breath."
>Coach: "What did you think at the time or afterwards?"
>Mr. Smith: "You can do it, old boy (laughing)."
>Coach: "And what would John Wayne say?"
>Mr. Smith: "(proudly) Well done!"
>Coach: "How did you wife react?"
>Mr. Smith: "She felt really proud! And I got a special treat in the evening!"

11c What is different in situations where the difficulty appeared less strong/was not there?

Here the attention has to be directed to the factors, that will make a big difference between success and failure in difficult situations. After the realisation of successes in a detailed description it will be much easier for your partner to reflect the differences to the current difficult situation.

Case example 11c

Coach: "What was different when you told your superior what you wanted to tell him?"
Mr. Smith: "There was a fixed guide-line for our business goals. Normally the boss persuades us to accept his opinion."
Coach: "And your personal safety was the decisive factor for your statement?"
Mr. Smith: "Yes, indeed."

III. 12. QUESTIONS ABOUT RESERVES AND ABILITIES

12A What skills did you use, to turn the relevant situation into success?
12B How did you manage that the described difficulty did not turn up?
12C How will you revive the activated reserves of that time?

If your partner sees the relevant facts for problems primarily in the surroundings ('I cannot achieve anything against my boss!') then it is necessary to strengthen his self-esteem, such that actions can be planned and executed, although the superior is ahead because of his superior status (position of power).

Therefore, e.g. the successful side of life could be assessed in a list showing the 10 biggest successes based on your skills and reserves.

… and now you!
Make a list of the 10 biggest successes in your life. Then add your skills and competence that enabled the successes. Please consider calmly how you could use this reservoir of talents for your current topic. Or follow C. SENGLER-ROST's recommendation and 'earth' yourself; stand by your skills in that you stand on your piece of paper commencing difficult actions or attacking difficult situations.

If the failure is referred to missing personal competence ('I am too stupid, too clumsy for this!' then it is important to recall one's own skills and reserves in a conversation.

12A   What skills did you use, to turn the relevant situation into success?

We often forget that we have already succeeded in similar situations like the current one. This surely has something to do with the way our brain functions. Therefore, it is no coincidence that the majority of our thinking includes open tasks, as they give us an unpleasant feeling.

CASE EXAMPLE 12A

Coach: "Which skills were there in that situation?"
Mr. Smith: "Courage, impudence and the ability to take my courage
   in both hands."

If your partners should be unable to name their abilities or differences between successful and unsuccessful situations, then it is in the advisor's competence to lead them along using proposing questions ('What do you think, does it have something to do with your ability to take stress or assert yourself ?') or to give them questions as a task.

The psychologist ALFRED ADLER calls the feeling that binds itself to failures and fears and comes up prior to a successful coping with a situation, a feeling of minority. In his opinion it acts as drive. Upon the successful coping of situations a feeling of superiority comes up. It is necessary to activate the countless successes, that we can all recall from our memory, to develop a feeling of superiority in a difficult situation and 'straighten' the picture we have of ourselves.

These are the reserves we hold within ourselves:

• Pictures of successes and the attached pleasant feelings!

• Skills we used then and we can use again at any time!

It is furthermore necessary, to activate already existing solution strategies – plus the pleasant feeling of superiority regarding that situation. In other words it is important to remember trouble-free times, where we coped. 'We have always found a solution!'

12B How did you manage that the described difficulty did not turn up?

If the memory of a certain situation is activated it can be described in detail. Insights in details, thoughts and feelings are possible, which offer initial signs to solutions for current situations. Here lie the keys to open currently still locked doors. It is important to hear which facts were especially helpful in the past situation.

CASE EXAMPLE 12B

Coach: "How did you manage not to submit, but speak up?"
Mr. Smith: "One has to speak up once, saying what one thinks is right. It wasn't that difficult."

> Look inside yourself! You will find a source of Good, that never stops bubbling as long as you don't stop digging.
>
> MARK AUREL

So please dig and ask how one can re-activate the discovered skills and reserves. Because if you can identify what you did 'wrong' and what you did 'right' then you will know the factors according to rule 1 and 2, which you can leave out or have to use to reach your goal.

12C How will you revive the activated reserves of that time?

You or your partner can also visualise the ABC of your reserves or skills in a 'reserve' pot. You can ask your partner to visualise the described skills and reserves, to recall them to his/her mind. You can leave it up to the expert of his/her solutions to decide if he/she wants to use the linguistic or visual form, or if he/she would rather use an empty piece of paper or the model 'reserve' pot, or if he/she wants to do the task here and now or at home.

... and now you!
Please insert all your skills usable in your current situation into the reserve pot!

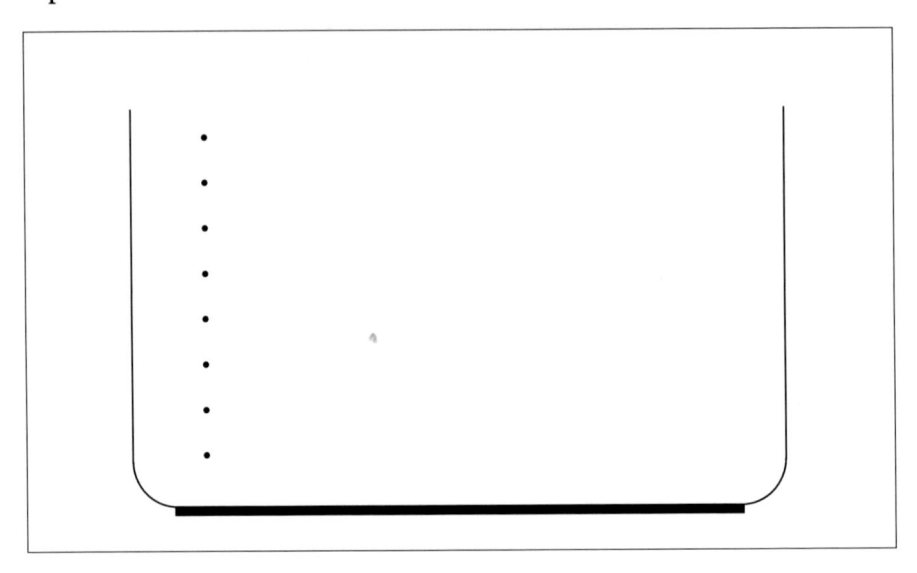

Case example 12c

 Coach: "What will you presently do to revive the activated reserves of that time?"
Mr. Smith: "Well, I will make an appointment with my superior."
 Coach: "What will you say, which goals do you want to agree on?"
Mr. Smith: "Instead of this invasion I'd rather have daily meetings. I like the principle of the open door and would like to arrange that my superior introduces this for everyone."

The energy and clarity about the goals arising thus, can be used to take the first step on the ladder to reach the goals and to determine the full benefit of ones skills.

III. 13. QUESTIONS ABOUT THE NEXT STEP

13A Any flight of stairs, however long, begins with the first step.
What will you do to get one step higher on the scale?
How long will it take you?

13B How will you or anyone else notice that you stepped up on the scale?

13C If you are now on step X on the scale, where would you want to be in a week or a month? What exactly will be different? How will you or others notice the difference?

Solution-oriented working means approaching a goal step by step.

**Do not be afraid to slow down!
But be afraid to stop!**

FROM CHINA

If the goal is known and we are aware of the talents we used for past successes, we can also use these for the first step. The ABC for the first step is as follows:

13A Any flight of stairs, however long, begins with the first step.
What will you do to get one step higher on the scale?
How long will it take you?

… and now you!
Insert your is-condition as well as the first step into the right column of the following scale.

```
10 = if everything runs smoothly        10
 9                                       9
 8                                       8
 7                                       7
 6 = my next step                        6
 5 = where I am now                      5
 4                                       4
 3                                       3
 2                                       2
 1 = if everything goes wrong            1
```

Case example 13a

Coach: "You'll have a discussion with your superior. Wonderful! How can you use your talents and the courage if you feel sure of yourself, to explain to your superior that you want to arrange daily consultations and the principle of the open door for daily and ritualrules of communication? On the scale, that is the gauge showing how close you got to the wonder, you stand between 3-4. What do you wish to start with to get one step higher on the scale?"

Mr. Smith: "Well, I would have to grab him first!"

∼

13b How will you or anyone else notice that you stepped up on the scale?

… and now you!
Outline your replies.

The partner describes positive changes and the attached pleasant feelings. This step also has a pleasant effect and there are no thoughts of fear of a possible failure, which rather unsure or problem-focussing people would feel prior to a difficult situation.

CASE EXAMPLE 13B

Coach: "How will you or e.g. Kasulke notice, that you have moved up a step on the scale?"
Mr. Smith: "Well the appointment will have been made, the boss will also be aware of the topics and Kasulke will be surprised about my decision!"
Coach: "The fact that you have made an appointment for a personal discussion with your superior brings you a step up, isn't that so?" Then you're on …"
Mr. Smith: "… about 5!"

Any step however small, which was successful, takes you closer to your goal than the moaning that large steps are impossible.

Small deeds one puts into action, are better than planning large ones.

G. C. MARSHALL

13C If you are now on step X on the scale, where would you want to be in a week or a month? What exactly will be different? How will you or others notice the difference?

The three example questions for the ABC of the next step assist to realise that we can plan and change our life in varied ways within certain borders. Everybody has it in his/her power to make decisions. The energy that comes up with successes can be made available through a mental anticipation of the actions. The view into the solution world creates positive energy and at the same time avoids the unpleasant problem mood.

In a dialogue – also in an inner dialogue with ourselves – we can anticipate various possible reactions of other persons. By creating such a memory lane we are able to return to sentences that we memorised for this occasion, despite of the agitation we feel. This minimises the likelihood of a mental blockage. This method has already proven successful in the behavioural therapy of fears over some decades.

> A journey of 1000 miles also begins with the first step.
>
> Laotse

Case example 13c

Coach: "If you are on 5, where will you be if the discussion went according to your wishes?"
Mr. Smith: "Maybe on 8!"
Coach: "What will be different if you're on 8?"
Mr. Smith: "My boss accepted my opinion and will have had time for me. We'll greet each other in a friendly way and respect each other as equals, he won't express his superiority any longer."
Coach: "Who else will notice that something has changed?"
Mr. Smith: "Well, my wife, she'd be satisfied because I would be more satisfied and also calmer!"

III. 14. COMPLIMENTS AND HELPFUL QUESTIONS

14A Word acknowledgement: super, smashing, wonderful, fantastic, great, respect!
14B After what you have told me I would definitely believe that you are capable of doing it! What are the basic conditions if everything runs smoothly?
14C What do you need to increase your confidence to reach your goal? What would be helpful?

A central element of solution-orientation is the creation and keeping-up of a confident atmosphere in conversation. Mehlmann & Röse (2000) described it as 'helpful to accentuate any attempts clients have already carried out successfully in their solution area'. Within a solution discussion verbal acknowledgements can now be added to non-verbal acknowledgements in problem discussions. From my experience it is more pleasant to let success seem more successful with verbal compliments, than to heighten problem focussing with verbal acknowledgements.

You will surely have enough examples for verbal acknowledgements and the following survey only points out the conscious use of those within the area of solution.

14A Word acknowledgement: super, smashing, wonderful, fantastic, great, respect!

These respectful and honestly meant responses at a certain time reduce the fears of change, as it underlines the naturalness you use assuming that you and your partner are naturally capable to get away from the problems and reach the set goals.

> A friendly word does not cost anything, but still it is the most precious gift.
>
> D. du Maurier

If you have learned about the previous successes and you now know all about the solution strategies and planned actions until a certain date, you can strengthen your partner's feelings of self-confidence with compliments and at the same time ask about the confidence of reaching the planned step.

CASE EXAMPLE 14A

> Coach: "Your wife is satisfied? But that is a fantastic additional benefit!"

∽

> 14B After what you have told me I would definitely believe that you are capable of doing it! What are the basic conditions if everything runs smoothly?

Sometimes a change in the surroundings can help to approach a goal. Therefore, it is important to find success factors within the basic condition.

CASE EXAMPLE 14B

> Coach: "With what you told me I can predict that you'll manage. Will the basic conditions also have changed when you reach the wonderful condition?"
> Mr. Smith: "I would have requested a new computer, and well, I would have got it."

∽

> 14C What do you need to increase your confidence to reach your goal? What would be helpful?

The question 'What do you need …' supersedes the problem-focussing question 'What stops you …?' It is an open question and thinking about the response gives several possibilities to reflect on the assistance from the surroundings or the activation of ones own reserves and skills and to systematically plan necessary actions.

Case example 14c

Coach: "What do you need for your confidence to reach 9?"
Mr. Smith: "Well, a good question! What do I need? The certainty that I represent the right view (smiling) and a day with a good mood."

III. 15. EXCEPTIONAL FORMS OF COMMUNICATION

15A Paradox communication
15B Provocative communication
15C Exaggeration

This chapter comprises of solution-oriented questions diverging from the usual way as well as the successful methods of conflict solutions for couples and groups.

> *Humour is not a gift from the brain but a gift from the heart.*
>
> LUDWIG BÖRNE

The paradox communication uses creativity and humour as an important source of human reserves of energy to distance oneself from the problem.

15A What could you do or think to feel even worse?

An important condition for this method is a good relation between the partners. In which case paradox questions turn out to be a good alternative to overcome inhibitive levels and to talk about goals and solutions. This method, also known as 'paradox intention', comprises of the request to imagine the situation as even worse and the problem as even stronger, this method is also used by FRANKL and WATZLAWICK amongst others. To express mainly socially unwelcome things produces a kind of release. Although this method could not be confirmed scientifically in all situations, it enables one to create a distance to ones problems as integral part of the solution-orientation. Sometimes an amusing distance to the problem causes an inner release.

Case example 15a

> Coach: "I'm glad to see you so confident! Now an unusual question: What could you do or think to reduce your confidence? How would it be possible to get your scaredy-cat to be big and strong?"
> Mr. Smith: "If I would listen to the scaredy-cat and consider a notice!"

15b Provocative communication

The American psychologist Frank Farelli (1963) developed the provocative style. Farelli had had enough to always be understanding and sympathetic with clients. With the help of the provocative style the problem-oriented mood should be interrupted and reserves set free. Required are:

- an intact relationship between the partners, characterised by the principles fairness, sincerity and respect of the human dignity,
- that both can laugh about a phrase. The phrases should be said with an eye twinkle.

Example: 'I always find the wrong job!' Preposterous re-interpretation: 'Some people have the talent to find exactly the most stupid job out of a 1000 jobs!'

This statement can relax your partner's train of thoughts and help to develop solutions. Your partner should be able to laugh and get a distanced access to his problem.

Case example 15b

> Coach: "And? Will you let your scaredy-cat out, which would rather run off, instead of having a difficult discussion?"
> Mr. Smith: "Me and scaredy-cat? Pah. What I intend to do I will do!"

15C Exaggeration

The above outlined exaggerations: 'always', 'never', 'all', 'nobody' can be taken up by the listener. If one of the four is used one can alternatively use all four for re-interpretation, according to Ellis, Meichenbaum or Satir and hold up a strongly excessive mirror.

>Example 1: 'I never get along with the pupils!'
>Exaggeration: 'You never get along. The pupils always do what they want. Nobody listens to you. Everybody is disobedient and inattentive.'
>
>Example 2: 'What should I do with the pupils?'
>Exaggeration: 'Why don't you kill them all, then you'll have peace!'

This foolish advice will lead your partner to the understanding that he/she cannot expect any advice from you and that he/she him/herself has the responsibility for his/her solutions.

>### Case example 15C
>
>Coach: "You'll never manage to throw your scaredy-cat out!"
>Mr. Smith: "Oh yes, this time I will! Bet you?!"
>
>… and now you!
>Finish your train of thought regarding your fears. Write down a story where everything you did went wrong. Imagine all possible catastrophes in detail!

Here I wish to get your attention to an important cognition in communication psychology and the solution findings, the knowledge of which is an important method to reach inner human goals not only for Mr. Smith but also for yourself. The expectation of communication is only fulfilled if all involved parties have satisfied their needs and have reached success suiting their individual interests. GORDON (1989, 1993) describes how we try to satisfy our needs via communication.

Messages according to Gordon

The sender encodes his message in certain characters, which are sent in form of language, music, gestures etc (medium) over certain channels (eye, ear, feeling). The recipient decodes this message, reacts according to his needs, feelings and perceptive tendencies and turns into a sender. This course of communication comprises of a constant change of roles and at the same time the talent to listen, think and form messages. The following groups of messages can be distinguished:

1. Hidden messages

These are statements put 'in a roundabout way' rather indirectly stating ones own wishes, feelings and needs.

Examples: 'It is draughty …' or
 'Somebody should do some shopping …' or
 'Does one do that?'

Also irony - to say the opposite of what one thinks - and to hide behind standard phrases ('One doesn't do that') - describe the tendency to hide true feelings. This makes it difficult to reach the goal in communication: the recipient has a lot of possibilities to give an evasive answer ('There is no draught here/I don't feel the draught') or to return the ball ('Then go and do some shopping'). This message encourages the need to find appreciation and respect in a group (with jokes).

2. Solution messages

With a solution message the sender tells the recipient what he has to do or leave.

Examples: 'Close the door! Leave it! Go to your room!'

These messages are used in military institutions (orders and obedience as communicative principles). They are marked by the imperative. The recipient knows exactly what to do. On the other side this means that the recipient can hardly satisfy his/her own need for power as well as his/her striving for self-realisation.
One possibility how persons involved can communicate on an equal (power) level is described by the principle of 'asking instead of ordering'. The same facts are now phrased as a question, though the partner may deny this.

'Could you please close the door?' just has a different tone and shows that there exists an intact relationship with respect for each other or is being striven for.

3. You-messages

You-messages are statements, holding information about the other person.

Example: 'Did you grow up in a tent. Can't you do anything right?'

Sometimes you-messages are used as praise (see Chapter 14A) but often to 'judge, condemn, rate, moan, abuse, mock, embarrass, belittle, humiliate, polemicise, accuse, warn, admonish, threaten, moralise etc - all hiding ones own needs and pushing the other to adopt a defensive position' (HOBMAIR, 1997). Normally, the recipient decides whether it is a you-message or not. Such a hidden message meant as a joke ('Did you get up with the wrong leg this morning?') could be understood as a you-message and evoke a corresponding reaction ('So what? What concern is that of yours?').
The relationship of the persons involved in the communication can also be analysed through messages. In a bad relationship you-messages and hidden

messages are the rule and solution-messages are mostly boycotted. ('Take the rubbish bin out!', 'Do it yourself'). The goal of the message (a regulation of factual questions, an intact relationship, satisfied needs) is mostly not achieved.

Whilst you-messages could have a disastrous effect on the recipient's imagination of him/herself, because you doubt his/her character, reject him/her as a person, emphasise his/her inadequacies and judge his/her personality, there is also a form of communication that leads to a profit for everybody involved. The winner-winner principle is based on the complete abstaining from you-messages and to formulate I-messages.

4. I-messages

I-messages are statements about my own feelings and needs.

Examples: 'I feel comfortable with you. I have got a real problem at the moment. I don't know how to carry on. I feel small and helpless.'

These statements are a form of you-messages (e.g. You're making me furious. You're getting me down. You are a …') are an attack on the person the sender makes responsible.

I-messages on the other hand get the other to think about his/her own mistakes. The adrenaline level remains low, which decreases the danger to reply in you-messages. Furthermore, nothing is clearer than a statement about ones own feelings. In my opinion the ability to speak freely about ones feelings shows strength. The following examples should explain the difference between you-messages and I-messages:

You-message	I-message
"You're talking nonsense!"	"I don't understand, what you mean."
"You're talking too much, you egoist, be quiet for once!"	"I would like to tell you something too."
"You're mean and inconsiderate!"	"What you just said hurt me plenty."
"You're always twisting my words!"	"I feel misunderstood."

Recognise the communication-barriers:

1. Hidden messages:
   Distracting, teasing; sayings, wise sayings; irony, sarcasm.

2. Solution-messages:
   Ordering, tasking, making proposals.

3. You-messages:
   Warning, admonishing, threatening; moralising; judging, criticising, nagging; reproaching, insulting; praising.

… **and now you!**
To recognise and rephrase communication barriers.

Solution Page 135

1. Statement	2. Recognising	3. Rephrasing
The superior says to his employee:		Your recommendation of an I-message or principle: *'asking instead of telling'*
You should have refrained	*Threat –> you-message*	*I don't think from this that's right!*
You will do the archiving now!		
You're saying this, because you're angry …		
Only bad employees think that.		
Don't ever do this again!		
Think first, then talk …		
You are really a mean bastard.		

The goal of this conduct is for all persons involved to feel as winners. To set up a winner-winner situation, co-operation is important. According to the Harvard concept (FISHER et al., 1997) it is therefore very important not to haggle but to concentrate on the interests and needs. The essential element is not to haggle for right or wrong, TV or cinema in the evening, or 2.4 or 4.2 percent increase in wages during discussions for rate agreements.

Successful negotiations should be featured in an atmosphere of openness where ones own interests and needs are discussed. As the authors pointed out this way co-operation rises in the main and the disadvantages of uneasy compromises are overcome. You will know for yourself that a compromise leaves at least one party feel uncomfortable upon conclusion. Sometime later the negotiations will have to be started again and satisfaction will only prevail if both feel to be winners. The time up to a satisfying conclusion is not optimally used by a compromise.

A consent, the inner yes to a negotiated compromise, means not to moan about what is missing, but to support the not optimal agreement for 100%.

SPRENGER (1998, page 219) writes:
"A consent does not look on what is missing but on what is possible. This also includes not to reach an agreement. If you cannot reach a solution workable for both sides then agree to differ, thus enabling you to put all energy into new tasks. But if a 'yes' only follows to end an unpleasant situation (flight) or to do another person a favour or because you believe that anything else would lead to other dreadful consequences you will make life difficult for yourself."

Strategies in battle, marked by the use of tricks taking advantage of authority, do not encourage co-operation but are a part of compromises.

The most harmful strategy is flight. Whilst in earlier times flight actually meant moving away from the situation, today we experience more and more cases of 'an inner withdrawal' in working life. In daily working life this means one is problem-focussing and not supporting ones own interests. Instead unpleasant facts are often 'swallowed', shown in many forms of stomach and back aches, 'crutches' like misuse of alcohol and tablets as well as aggression and other psychosomatic illnesses.

Only discussions held in an open atmosphere can create co-operation. A possible way to discuss criticism or conflicts is the 'coffee chat'.

In a coffee chat all parties agree to sit down in a quiet moment with a cup of coffee and to talk about facts that did not run well. To avoid problem-focussing and keep the adrenaline level as low as possible I would advise the following procedure:

1st Phase: compliment = positive I-message
"During the past weeks we had a good co-operation with customer X, which I liked very much!"

2nd Phase: description of the situation
"I didn't like one situation. The customer asked me a question but before I could reply you did."

3rd Phase: I-message
"At that moment I felt like a beginner. That annoyed me!"

4th Phase: To hear the other's opinion
"How did you feel about it?" Ask the other person for his/her view. But do not start to defend yourself or get upset. Respect the other's view and try to find a common ground.

5th Phase: Wish for the future
"I'm happy about your engagement but I do not wish to be interrupted by you. If I'm asked something and can't think of anything, I will turn to you or you can continue my thoughts when I've finished."

6th Phase: Get a consent
"Is that alright with you?"

Get a consent. An arrangement where the partner has not given his/her clear yes, is not a mutual arrangement and would probably not function. This procedure leads to arrangements that are often kept and the partner is not pushed for an explanation and into a defensive position.

If you as listener notice that you begin to get upset, then just try to pay attention to the other's words, to be able to repeat them. Look forward, not back and remain hard on the case and soft to the people.

… and now you!
Coffee chat – choose a problem and phrase your feelings and wishes to your partner

---

1 st   Phase – compliment:

2 nd   Phase – description of situation:

3 rd   Phase – I-message:

4 th   Phase – Hear the others opinion:

5 th   Phase – Wish for the future:

6th   Phase – get consent:

III. 16. SOLUTION-ORIENTATION IN THE LANGUAGE

16A The critical dialogue (of ones own rules and values)
16B Reframing – Rephrasing
16C What will you do (think) instead?

To speak and think – what have these complex procedures to do with each other? Simply said: they depend on each other. We (sometimes) say what we think and we think about (not always) what we say. If we talk about our problems we think about our problems and often get into a 'problem mood'. If we think about our dreams and conversations that went well, we will get into raptures and into a motivated solution mood. Therefore, it is very important not only to pay attention to the content of a discussion but also to the choice of thoughts and words.

ELLIS (1977) developed a comprehensive system of changing inhibiting thoughts, similar to Satir's approach. According to Ellis many problems exist because people demand to be successful and respected, insisting on fair treatment or dictating that life should be more amusing.

16A The critical dialogue

Whilst talking to oneself it is necessary to question ones own thoughts. Instead of a monologue a dialogue with oneself should lead to dissociation to increase the understanding of others, to a critical attitude of oneself and therefore to a change of this attitude. A critical dialogue of inner 'must' thoughts ('It must be like this!') leads to a change of thoughts which again shows in new potentials of self-esteem.

Example: A critical dialogue about the topic 'punctuality'. "Why do I always have to be on time anyway? The others aren't either. But I don't like to wait. I don't want others to have to wait. That's just not done! (Rule herein: I should not let anybody wait). Well mostly I have to wait as I'm early or on time. The others don't think it is important. Well it isn't really. In the past my parents put great store on punctuality. But today ... well. Whilst I'm waiting I can do something useful. Then I'll have something nice to do and am distracted. I do not have to be annoyed about others not being on time. I'll have the chance to do something else. Punctuality is important but I can stand minor delays of 15 minutes."

... and now you!
Lead your own critical dialogue here.

༄

CASE EXAMPLE 16A

Coach: "Please lead a critical dialogue about the topic: The scaredy-cat in me!"
Mr. Smith: "Well, I've always been rather a scared child, a lot of people mocked me. But there were also situations when I was so angry that I got into fights. So I wasn't always like that. Later on I often ducked my head. On hindsight this didn't bring me as many advantages as I thought. On one side I remain silent and on the other I let out. But the wrong persons get the blame. That is not right as I open further problems, which get on my nerves. It would be better if I could say my piece straight away. And to the right person!"

༄

16B Reframing – Rephrasing

The ability to re-evaluate behaviour and to revise traditional views by rephrasing statements has to be used consistently for oneself and others to prevent the emergence of blockages.

Example 1 should explain the working of rephrasing

Person A: 'A person in my area often interrupts me and gets into the centre of attention.'

Person B: 'Which positive skills does the person show at that time?'

Rephrasing Person A:
'Well he/she can assert him/herself and reach his/her goals most times.'

The dialogue stimulates reflection: How can I use the positive part of a seemingly negative feature to reach a change of thoughts?

Rephrasing exercise 1 for you:

'My boss is not open for such suggestions.'

Solution-oriented rephrasing:

Example 2: 'The child is naughty.'

Problem-focussing continuation:
'Yes, terrible. Nowadays parents have not much authority any more!'

Solution-oriented rephrasing:
'It has a mind of its own, maybe ...'

Rephrasing exercise 2 for you:

'My employee drops everything on time and immediately drives home to his family!'

Problem-focussed continuation:

Solution-oriented rephrasing:

Furthermore, the possibility arises to escort our partner out of the world of moaning into the world of solution.

Example 3: 'After this terrible incident the progress was only slow.'

Problem-focussing continuation:
'What was terrible?' 'What slowed it down?'

Solution-oriented rephrasing:
'What was better afterwards?'
'How did you notice the progress?'

Rephrasing exercise 3 for you:

'I just don't manage to stop smoking at the moment.'

Problem-focussed continuation:

Solution-oriented rephrasing:

As language influences thinking, it is important to check the language on its problem contents. If a person uses many negative terms, it is important to escort him/her into the world of success by rephrasing them into positive associated terms. This is explained in exercise 4:

Example 4: 'Everybody avoids me.'

The opposite of avoiding is 'to wish to speak to someone'.

To avoid = no desire to speak to someone

'Was there ever a situation when someone wished to speak to you?'

Example 5: 'Life is terrible.'

The opposite of terrible is 'nice'.

Terrible = not nice

The comparative of nice = nicer

'Are there times when life is nicer?'

Rephrasing exercise 4 for you:

'Everything is bad.'

1. The opposite

2. Bad = not

3. Comparative

4. Was there

The rephrasing of words with a negative association will succeed if you form the opposite and then deduce a comparative.

Case Example 16b

> Coach: "The opposite of anxiety is courage or certainty! Have there ever been situations where you felt more courage towards your superior?"
> Mr. Smith: "Yes in previous times I often opened my mouth but it didn't always go well!"
> Coach: "Can you recall when it did you good or even very good?"
> Mr. Smith: "Yes, that was about …"

Whilst working on the problem, there is always the possibility to interrupt the flow of thoughts with an internal – STOP! And to reflect if you are just listing problems and expect failures or if you choose a solution for your problem. Try to find your current situation in the following sketch. Are you on the left side or on the ascending line on the right hand side?

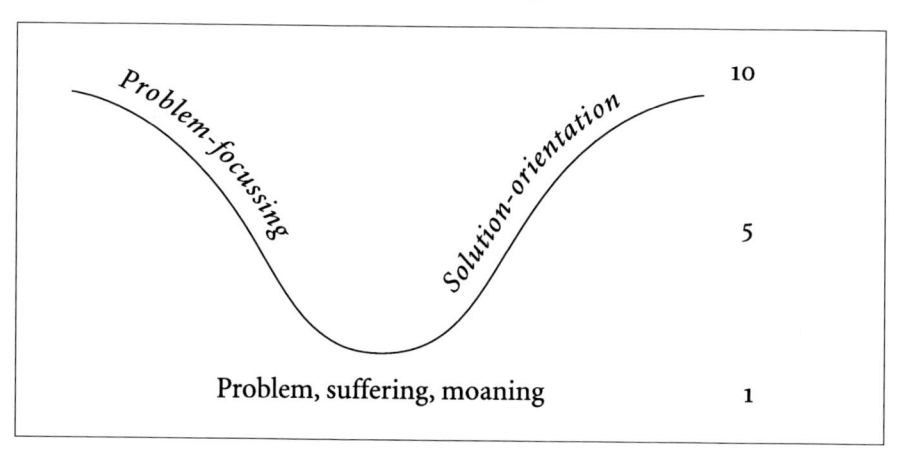

Problem-focussing   *Solution-orientation*   10

Problem, suffering, moaning   5

    1

Are you within an emotional hole, do not absorb it by further thinking about the problem point of view, but to the constructive part of change, the solution-orientation. This way you will climb towards the 10 on the scale. If you are in a conversation with someone who moans and moans, it is important to increase the other's perception that next to difficult times there surely also were times where difficulties had been sorted out successfully. For us it is also an advantage to look onto the parts of day and life that worked out after the stop!

You can change from the left to the right branch at any time, from moaning about something that does not work out towards acting in small steps to reach your goals being optimistic in advance!

In many cases your partners will formulate his/her own positive skills and reserves for the first time. This is even more important if one knows that speaking about it will construct reality. Talking and thinking influence our body in such a strong way that e.g. thoughts like: 'Oh Lord, the next wave of flue will surely grab me!' will cause a detectable decrease of anti bodies and according to a self fulfilling prophecy the condition one has predicted for oneself actually happens. Because people have this talent of self-influence, it is important to use these energies positively to reach a goal and to stop negative words leading to a blockage of actions.

Imagination comforts people over what they cannot be And humour comforts them over what they really are.

ALBERT CAMUS

16c What will you do (think) instead?

People often do not formulate their goals but what they do not want. But until all the things are formulated that should not be done, the pictures are revived about what should not happen, people have wasted a lot of time. Zest for life and physical strength.

CASE EXAMPLE 16C

Coach: "Instead of bearing your superior's 'assaults', what will you do?"
Mr. Smith: "I will make an arrangement with him. Then he can call me over the phone and maybe tell me the topic so I can prepare myself!"

The question: 'What will you do instead?' immediately pushes the energies into a solution-oriented way.

Examples:

'I never want to have such a boss!' 'How should your boss be instead?'
'I don't fancy Italian food today!' 'What would you fancy instead?'
'My wages should ot be as low as last time.' 'What would you think appropriate this time?'

... and now you!
Support the language of solution-orientation.

'I'll never recommend shares again.'

'I don't believe in one God.'

'I don't feel love for her any more.'

'I don't like this work any more.'

'I don't want to watch football.'

III. 17. EXERCISES FOR THE WEEKDAYS

17A On getting up in the morning please tell yourself how good the day on a scale of 1-10 will be. In the evening you can compare your prophecy with your assessment.

17B Please choose one day of next week and act as if the miracle had already happened, i.e. I explicitly ask you to act as if you could do what you want to do on those days. Note down your experience that made this day different to other days.

17C Please note down your benefit if everything remains as it is and your benefit if you have solved the problem. Put the relevant arguments in a list side by side.

In solution-oriented conversations it is standard to agree on an activity before parting.

Man has to help himself in this world.

J. H. Pestalozzi

Working with the following questions from the ABC of tasks will help you to find the pleasant sides of a day.

17A The prognosis-task:

On getting up in the morning please tell yourself how good the day on a scale of 1-10 will be. In the evening you can compare your prophecy with your assessment.

Please note down pleasant situations that brought your day towards 10 (very good). Also note down incidents that worsened (1) the day.

The next conversation will help to specifically use the found positive factors and to intensify them. The unpleasant situations are picked out as topic and tackled with the miracle question. You have the opportunity to try the miracle. For this day you will instruct yourself to act with optimism in advance as if the miracle for that day had already come true.

CASE EXAMPLE 17A

Coach: "We have talked about your goals and you have already mentioned what you want to do. To look what might make your day good or bad I want to give you a task. Okay?"
Mr. Smith: "Agreed!"
Coach: "If you get up tomorrow morning please tell yourself how good your day will be on a scale of 1-10. 10 means super, 1 means terrible and at the end of the day you'll look back to what was good and what was not so good and note down the facts that influenced your day.
Mr. Smith: "Okay and what day?"
Coach: "We'll meet again in a week. I would like to ask you to do this for every day of this week. Then we'll have a representative part of your life and we can work with the results!"
Mr. Smith: "Agreed!"

~

17B The 'to do as if' task:

Please choose one day of next week and act as if the miracle had already happened, i.e. I explicitly ask you to act as if you could do what you want to do on those days (MEHLMANN & RÖSE, 1999). Note down your experience that made this day different to other days (incidents, thoughts, feelings).

Above all, this form of solution-strategy is an advantage if you want to change something about yourself. Necessary for e.g. a diet or abstinence from a drug is the ability to say 'No' convincingly. This 'No' is real if you are able to say it with a good and proud feeling, without thinking how good something would taste at that moment. The miracle instead happened and you simply do not need the drug any more to confront daily conflicts. And this 'I am free' is a confirmation of the self-effectiveness and at the same time a commitment which strengthens itself.

If the topic is about the improvement of the relationship to another person, you can arrange the day such that you treat this person as a good friend. Imagine visually that the relationship would be free of strain and friction and the relationship to this person will be friendly.

- What will your friendly greeting look like?
- How will you behave during a discussion about work?
- How will you talk in a pleasant conversation by telephone?
- What will you do for your colleague/superior, what you have never done before?

CASE EXAMPLE 17B

Coach: "I also want to ask you to pick a day of next week and to act as if the miracle had already happened. On that day you will act as if your superior fully accepts you and you will act with courage and also maybe take a little risk, without covering yourself. How do you think you would be abe to manage this?"

Mr. Smith: "One day of the next five? (pause) Yes that would be exciting, (smiling) yes I think that would be nice, but would I do it?"

Coach: "One day during the week. Would you manage?"

Mr. Smith: "Yes, I should think so."

Coach: "Sure? How sure on a scale of 1-10?"

Mr. Smith: "About 8! Yes, I know, you´ll now want to know how I could move to 9!"

Coach: "(laughing) Excellent, Mr. Smith! Very solution-oriented!"

Mr. Smith: "First I will imagine this wonderful condition again and the get going."

Coach: "That is a good decision!"

Surely, this task is not easy but appealing, as it will cause reactions in your surroundings that might lead to a discussion about the relationship. To set up the task it is important to agree on the contents and the time frame. This creates external motivation which then helps to overcome the inner inhibition level. In case the inhibition levels are so high that it would be impossible to leave the problem-focussing, you can ask the benefit-question!

17c The benefit-task:

Please note down your benefit if everything remains as it is and your benefit if you have solved the problem. Put the relevant arguments in a list side by side. This task gives your partners the possibility to visualise the benefit of changes and to compare them with the benefit of the current situation. As this is mostly low, the result assists to step towards solution-orientation.

CASE EXAMPLE 17C

> Coach: "If any doubts should come up whether or not you can manage the 'to-do-as-if' task, I would advise the benefit-task for support."
> Mr. Smith: "And – what is the benefit-task?"
> Coach: "Well, you write down the benefit from a change and list the benefit if everything remains as it is next to it."
> Mr. Smith: "No, no. I donít need that, the benefit is clear to me!"

III. 18. FINAL QUESTIONS

18A If our discussion was like a dinner with hors d'œuvre, main menue and dessert, ...
18B The scale questions to measure your satisfaction of the discussion
18C You have phrased your goal and the first step towards this goal, ...

It is important to understand your partner's mood as this will be a decisive factor whether or not the conversation will be continued or ended. I chose various possibilities that address various senses.

18A If our discussion was like a dinner with hors d'œuvre, main menue and dessert, ...

... where are we now?
... how did it taste, was it properly spiced?
... would you like to order anything else?
... what would you like to tell me, the cook, about the meal?

CASE EXAMPLE 18A

Coach: "Well, if you haven't got any more questions I hope you'll be successful with the conversion of your goals and your two tasks, the to-do-as-if task and the prognosis-task."
Mr. Smith: "Thank you. No, no more questions!"
Coach: "I just thought about a final one: If our discussion was like a meal with hors d'œuvre, main course and dessert, how did you like it?"
Mr. Smith: "Delicious (smiling). Especially the main course with the miracle question and the questions after the opinion of others. That was a good filet. Well spiced and not grilled too long. I like being cooked for like this!"
Coach: "Thank you for your response."

18B The scale questions to measure your satisfaction of the discussion

> Scale of satisfaction:
>
> How satisfied are you on a scale of 1-10, whereby 10 means very satisfied and 1 means very dissatisfied.

CASE EXAMPLE 18B

Coach: "How satisfied do you feel about todays discussion on a scale of 1-10, whereby 10 means very satisfied and 1 very dissatisfied?"
Mr. Smith: "Very satisfied 9-10. I would like to thank you. I feel a lot better!"

If the feedback is not 9 or 10 (= very well) it would be in the interest of an improvement of ones own skills to ask: Let's assume you had assessed the conversation at 10? What would we have done differently?

∼

18C You have phrased your goal and the first step towards this goal. When will we discuss that you have made this first step?

The reply to this question also concludes the discussion about solution with a commitment as regards to time and content. If our partners do not have any more questions or do not wish to discuss any further topics, then the solution discussion is finalised.

Case example 18c

Coach: "You have already phrased your goals to have a discussion with your superior. When will we discuss that this step was successful?"
Mr. Smith: "Next week about the same time?"
Coach: "Agreed. Good bye and good luck Mr. Smith!"

III. 19. LEAD-IN QUESTIONS TO THE NEXT DISCUSSION

19A What was the result of the tasks you wished to complete?
19B What has changed to the better since our last discussion?
19C What would you like to discuss today?

To complete tasks between appointments for discussion makes it clear to the partner that he/she can and has to do something to gain his/her goals. The lead-in into the resultant discussion will almost automatically deal with the coping of the given tasks.

19A What was the result of the tasks you wished to complete?

This question aims at making somebody conscious of the changes. Even if the facts (e.g. the monthly salary after ones approach to the superior for a rise) did not improve, theinterpretation of these facts can be totally different. With regards to problem-focussing this can lead to sleeplessness and a decrease of work dedication, but it can also be used as prove of courage and aid to decision-making for the oncoming working life.

CASE EXAMPLE 19A

Coach: "Welcome, Mr. Smith. What was the result of your task and the discussion with your superior?"
Mr. Smith: "Well, a lot better than I would have thought …"

~

19B What has changed to the better since our last discussion?

Solution-orientation is always also client-orientation. The expert for the solutions of his/her needs always has the right to choose the topic, product or form of service that will meet the fulfillment of his/her needs. In a discussion we should therefore leave out our own need to choose a topic and offer a maximal freedom of choice to our partner, so he/she can 'extinguish' what is preying on his/her mind.

Case example 19b

Coach: "What has improved since our last conversation?"
Mr. Smith: "First of all my superior and I had a conversation. Each morning we meet to make daily appointments, marvellous!"

Here perception is led to positive changes.

Life is what you make it.

Sallust

~

19c What would you like to discuss today?
     On a scale of 1-10, ...

     ... where are you now?
     ... where will you be after the discussion?
     ... what will be different?

Case example 19c

Coach: "On a scale of 1-10 whereas 10 is the wonderful condition, where are you at the moment, Mr. Smith?"
Mr. Smith: "Definitely on 9!"
Coach: "Wonderful, I'm delighted. If you reached 10 after our discussion what would be different?"
Mr. Smith: "Well, everything works out fine with my superior. Maybe, well yes, Kasulke, he now gets on my nerves with his calls. If I'd find a plan I'd be on 10 after this discussion!"
Coach: "Well then, let's get going, I'd like to put a perhaps unusual question to you. Let's assume that a miracle happened overnight ...!"

This question automatically makes a connection to the beginning of the solution-discussion (9A), the cycle of solution-oriented communication can commence again.

Solution-oriented communication shows an integrated way to speak about problems as well as to include the search for a solution. The main emphasis of the first conversation lies on the understanding of the whole situation including thoughts and feelings. This information is then used to show the double motivation for changes to the partner:

From problem to solution:

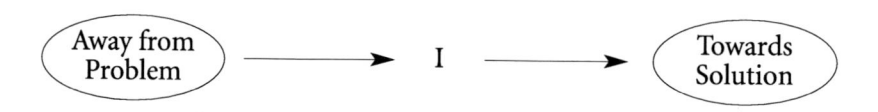

$$\boxed{\text{Away from Problem}} \longrightarrow I \longrightarrow \boxed{\text{Towards Solution}}$$

Solution-orientation for everybody just means that it is up to YOU to get away from the unpleasant side effects of problems but instead to use the precise vision of the solution as an attractive goal. It is up to YOU to change your basic position: from the self perception of a problem bearer to the self-effectiveness of a (more often) solution-oriented person.

I hope you'll enjoy yourself!

And please do not forget:

WITHIN CERTAIN LIMITS EVERYTHING IS POSSIBLE!

You have the possibility to alter the ABC of change to an ABCD of change, by adding your favourite question or a further successful question about your taste and language style.

Check list for the solution discussion

9. Questions to goals and future

9A When you retire to bed tonight, a fairy will come with her magic stick and everything we spoke about, every problem has found a solution. As you were asleep you won't know that the miracle has happened! So as you wake up tomorrow morning …

… how will you initially notice that the miracle has happened?
… what is different than normally?
… who else would notice? And how?

9B Assume we would meet again in a year and discuss this topic and how you managed to gaincontrol.

How will you have noticed that you have managed to reach your goal? Who else will have noticed (how)? What was different?

9C What exactly are your occupational and private goals?

9D _____

10. Scale questions

10A Please imagine a scale of 1-10, whereas 10 stands for the wonderful condition of the goal you just described. 1 stands for nothing happened. Where between 1 and 10 would you evaluate yourself today?

10B How confident do you feel about reaching your described goal? If you are totally sure, you'll keep all 10 stones. If you are totally unsure, you'll push all stones away, in between you can grade!

10C How many exceptions of the problem, i.e. successful experiences, were there? 10 stands for a lot of successes and 1 for only a few successes; you can grade in between!

10D _____

11. Questions about successful exceptions of the problem

11A When in the past has it been better?

11B Please describe a successful situation!

11C What is different in situations where the difficulty appeared less strong/was not there?

11D _____

12. Questions to reserves and abilities

12A What skills did you use, to turn that situation into success?

12B How did you manage that the described difficulty did not turn up?

12C How will you revive the activated reserves of that time?

12D _____

13. Questions to the next step

13A Any flight of stairs, however, long begins with the first step. What will you do to get one step higher on the scale? How long will it take you?

13B How will you or anyone else notice that you stepped up on the scale?

13C If you are now on step X on the scale:
Where would you want to be in a week or a month?
What exactly will be different? How wil you do it?
How will you or others notice the difference?

13D _____

14. Compliments and helpful questions

14A A word acknowledgement: super, smashing, wonderful, fantastic, great, respect!

14B After what you have told me I would definitely believe that you are capable of doing it! What are the basic conditions if everything runs smoothly?

14C What do you need to increase your confidence that you will reach your goal? What would be helpful?

14D _____

15. Exceptional forms of communication

15A What can you do or think to make yourself feel worse?

15B Provocative questions: Are you too stupid?

15C You will never manage that!

15D _____

16. Solution-orientation in the language

16A The critical dialogue (of ones own rules and values)

16B Reframing - Rephrasing

16C What will you do (think) instead?

16D _____

17. Exercises for the weekdays

17A On getting up in the morning please tell yourself how good the day on a scale of 1-10 will be. In the evening you can compare your prophecy with your assessment

17B Please choose one day of next week and act as if the miracle had already happened, i.e. I explicitly ask you to act as if you could do what you want to do on those days. Note down your experience that made this day different to other days.

17C Please note down your benefit if everything remains as it is and your benefit if you have solved the problem. Put the relevant arguments in a list side by side.

17D _____

18. Final questions

18A If our discussion was like a dinner with hors d'œuvre, main menue and dessert, ...

   ... where are we now?
   ... how did it taste?
   ... would you like to order anything else?
   ... what would you like to tell me, the cook, about the meal?

18B The scale questions to measure your satisfaction of the discussion

18C You have phrased your goal and the first step towards this goal. When will we discuss that you have made this first step?

18D _____

19. Lead-in questions to the next discussion

19A What were the results of the tasks you wished to complete?

19B What has changed to the better since our last discussion?

19C What would you like to discuss today?
     On a scale of 1 to 10, ...

   ... where are you now?
   ... where will you be after the discussion?
   ... what will be different?

19D _____

The Arnold-Matrix

The following table shows which questions are most useful. They were given to a workgroup 'solution-oriented-coaching' by coaches of the Deutsche Bank AG.

The Arnold-Matrix

	Opening of the discussion	Discussion of the problem	Distance	Vision	Successful coping in the past	Transfer to the future
Invitation to discuss a problem	x					
Non-verbal acknowledgement	x	x	x	x	x	x
Questions to behaviour		x		x	x	
Questions to thoughts		x		x	x	
Questions to emotions		x		x	x	
Circular questions		x	x	x	x	x
Questions for coping		x			x	
De-focussing		x				
Commitment		x				x
Questions to goals and future		x			x	
Scale questions		x	x		x	x
Successful exceptions of the problem		x			x	
Reserves and abilities		x			x	
Questions about the next step						x
Verbal acknowledgement				x	x	x
Helpful questions		x	x			
Exceptional questions		x	x	x	x	x
Rephrasing		x	x		x	
Exercises		x	x		x	x
Final questions						x
Lead-in to the next discussion	x					

Questions about behaviour – Solution proposals on Page 31:

He nags.	*How does he nag? What does he say?* *Who does he talk to?* *What is he nagging about?* *When will the nagging stop?* *What should he do instead?* *Assuming he would do something else, how do you imagine this?*
One does not hear a good word.	*From whom?* *About who or what?* *What is a good word?* *Who should say something like that?*
My frustration increases.	*How does this show?* *Frustration about what?* *Frustration due to who?* *What do you mean with frustration?*
I will not go along with that any more!	*With what will you not go along any more?* *What will you do instead?*

Solution proposals for the task on Page 106:

Recognising and rephrasing of communication blockades.

List of communication blockades:

Hidden messages:
Distracting, teasing; sayings, wise sayings; irony, sarcasm.

Solution-messages:
Ordering, tasking, making proposals.

You-messages:
Warning, admonishing, threatening; moralising; judging, criticising, nagging; reproaching, insulting; praising.

The superior says to his employee:	Your recommendation of an I-message:
You should have refrained from that! (Threat –> you-message)	I don't think that's right!
You will do the archiving now! (Order –> solution-message)	Can you do the filing now, please? Thank you!
You're saying this, because you're angry … (Interpretation –> you-message)	I'm not sure why you're saying this. Could you please explain yourself?
Only bad employees think that. (Judging –> you-message)	I don't agree with your thoughts!
Das machen Sie nicht noch einmal. (Warning –> you-message)	I didn't like this! Would you please stop?
Think first, then talk … (Sayings –> hidden messages)	I'm of a different opinion.
You are really a mean bastard! (Insult –> you-message)	I'm angry about your behaviour.

IV. 10 MISTAKES AND 10 COGNITIONS

Mistake 1:
To remain within problem-focussing and to increase the problem-view ...

'Yes that is really most terrible, one can now only hang oneself', I recently heard an 'adviser' say. In spite of all my sympathy for the partner, this attempt to emphasize with somebody does not lead to any actions or encourage a change. This rather encourages to remain within a problem mood and also encourages to just carry on with what does not function. A repetition of problems often leads to the feelings that 'everything is bad, will always remain so and will never change'. Thinking thus develops into a self-fulfilling prophecy.

The things will remain as they are, if I think they will remain as they are. The power of our thoughts is much stronger than we assume they are. Of course I will feel ill, if I keep telling myself that I will surely feel ill soon. Nowadays it is even possible to measure that the quantity of antibodies in a body will decrease after such self-suggestion. Therefore, it is necessary to use the main part of acknowledgements and compliments for successful attempts in the past or to emphasise skills and reserves, which have lead to a successful coping with difficulties.

Cognition 1:
It is more pleasant to force descriptions of successfully solved situations. This encourages the motivation to formulate and strive for solutions.

Mistake 2:
To act as if there were no problems.
Unfortunately there would be no solutions either!

Thoughts with regards to the inner rule: 'Only others have problems' can of course lead to a denial of difficulties. Then the 'blind spot' has to be made visible prior to commencing changes.

Self-esteem will be protected but fears are only suppressed and the energies released by such fears are active and will turn up in manifold form e.g. as aggression, tantrums, lack of self-control or as stomach ulcers, back- and headaches.

Phrased differently – a suppression of feelings and expression of one's emotions will prevent a fulfillment of ones individual needs for a full and sensible purpose in life. The amount of positive social contacts lessens; therefore the amount of perceived respect and compliments in the environment lessens.

Solution-oriented communication creates a positive view to solutions, if you approach the 'wonderful' goal in small steps and make yourself aware of your own reserves and skills. Only if you discuss problems or activate your inner solution-orientation, the energy can be used constructively for solutions.

The 'visioned' solution creates inner sources of energy as e.g. the dream of ones own house. You can activate your goals in life any time, which will give you strength and motivation in difficult times.

Cognition 2:
The miracle question permits to speak about the realisation of solutions and thus solve problems without releasing the accompanying fears.

Mistake 3:

Decisions are made by those persons who have more power in our relationship – I let others make decisions over my life.

If we look at the system 'family' in a vast amount of situations the parents decide when what how is done. If they then use their power in form of rewards or announced punishments (and use the children's fears or wishes), there is the danger that children will internalise this orientation of reward and punishment as moral standard and will also act accordingly as adults. Instead it is important to lead a conversation where decisions are brought about, agreed on and endured together. This 'winner-winner-principle' is also necessary for any other systems that want to be successful in the long term.

The system of the agreements on goals in a business is based on the same principle. However, in the end a lot of employees let the suoperior decide on goals they had agreed on together, as he/she not only has the power but additionally the better rethorical skills. Here it is necessary to prepare oneself thoroughly and to develop one's own argzuments to strengthen one's own interests.

The strength of the whole group can even cut the superior's advantage of power.Therefore, the group would have to act as a unit and allocate articulation to every member.

During a conversation it would be an advantage if the advising partner holds back advice and attempts of manipulation, also if one's own needs wil not be satisfied optimal. On middle and longer terms the listeners will receive thanks for this role, as this will increase ones self-confidence and the believe in one's own effectiveness.

Cognition 3:

Everybody is capable to lead a solution-oriented conversation.
Every individual is demanded to represent his/her opinion.

Mistake 4:
Impatient listeners want to enter the world of solution too fast.

When will someone be ready for the miracle question? Are there any signs? If you as listener notice that descriptions of things that do not work out are repeated or the partners end their description, this is the first sign for his/her will to transfer into the solution-orientation. If you as listener have a clean picture of the situation and the topic, it is up to you to repeat what you have heard and to use the method of defocussing.

Of course you can also ask straight on if your partner is ready to put his/her energy into working on the solutions. This way you will remain within your partner's tempo. If you discover that the partner 'is not yet ready' and does not believe in his strength, a useful topic at this point of the conversation would be the use of tasks.

Cognition 4:
Only if your partner has expressed his/her will to change something, a transfer into the world of solution will be worthwhile.

~

Mistake 5:
The right question at the wrong time ...

A question as such cannot be right or wrong. But it can be very useful or completely out of place, depending on how and where it is placed in a conversation. Such the miracle question would remain unanswered, if it would be used too early on in the conversation. If you and your partner have dived into the world of solution, then questions to further problems could easily destroy the pleasant atmosphere and the motivated mood. If you use the submitted introduction you can categorise your partner's topics in your mind. This gives you space to understand the contact and put questions to important areas which have not yet been mentioned.

So there are times to ask questions about behaviour, thoughts and feelings accompanying a problem and times for solution-oriented actions. In the business world the efficiency of meetings strongly depends on everybody's actions. Mostly the responsibility for an efficient conclusion is passed on to the more powerful persons in the group; but whoever internalised a solution-oriented action, will always be able to establish solution-orientation within the group.

Cognition 5:
A submitted introduction is a useful element to develop a structured manner of action to solve problems and lead efficient discussions.

∽

Mistake 6:
All people think and act the same as I do!

People intuitively presume that all other people impose the same criteria regarding problem-solving, or the interpretation of human actions. One rule based on this train of thoughts is 'as a good listener and advisor I have to pass on the knowledge of my solutions'. If listeners do not make themselves aware of this rule, they run the risk to falsify information heards according to their own expectations (projective perception, e.g. 'All people think and act the same as I do') or to hear and see just what fits in their own expectations and needs (selective perception).

LAY (1994) presumes that 'in a normal discussion 50% of what is said is considerably altered as regards to content due to selection and projection.

'Therefore, it is necessary to set up an inner rule, which forbids us to offer our solution proposals to others unasked for. Often solution messages turn out to be inappropriate or as already having been carried out ñ but unsuccessfully. Whenever advice is burning our tongue, we should let it burn. An open question instead brings about the actions that have already been tried to find a solution, without hearing a 'No!' to our advice. As every 'No!' is a sign of lack of professionalism, because a basic rule of listening was violated; the rule that the partner is the expert for his/her own solutions. If a listener receives more 'Nos' this could have the effect that the partner does not feel his/her listener to be competent and as a result might not discuss anything more.

Cognition 6:
If an advise burns your tongue, let it burn!

Another rule says here that advice is also a blow, namely an assault on the self-effectiveness of our partner. If you ask open questions instead and increase your partner's parts of the discussion your partner will feel even more comfortable and motivated to strive for solutions.

Mistake 7:

To not really listen.

To listen is hard work. To concentrate on the other's as well as ones own thoughts and at the same time to grab the essential coherence, are a high strain to every listener with regards to concentration and persistence of perception and thinking. The solution-oriented approach releases the listener from the strain to find solutions for other people. Solution-oriented listeners believe that the partner as expert for his/her problems and solutions also find a discussion worthwhile if no advice is offered.

Especially for men this is hard to understand, as the naming of solutions is an integral part of their coping with conflicts, whilst women strive for a solution of conflicts via the exchange of information and a mutual view on things. I got the impression that men have even larger reserves to listen. Some training is needed to enforce this process. To repeat what was said, before I declare my position as well as giving I-messages (messages about my feelings) instead of you-messages (messages about the other person, after condescending and evaluating), present supports into the coping with conflicts in relationships (GORDON, 1989, amongst others) that have every successful effect (see also THURMAIER & ENGEL, 1994).

The solution-oriented start has an relieving effect, as it works with vivid visions and a pleasant emotional language. Thus dual form (image and language) relieve the code in ones memory, decreases the danger of selective and projective perception and the listener's image comes closer to the speaker's image. Due to its structure the ABC of change makes it possible to sort the heard contents, enquire about unheard circumstances and push forward the change by recalling memorised questions.

Cognition 7:

Solution-oriented communication relieves the listener and helps all others.

Mistake 8:
I can change others – I cannot change others!

1. If it is my opinion that I can change others, it is likely that I see my basic rules verified that others change due to a discussion with me. After the interaction my partners are different: the problem-view, the feelings, the cognition of goals and the ways to reach these goals.

2. If I believe that I cannot change others – an experience that couples make in many areas of their married life – many conclusions can be gained:

   a) I have no influence on these people,
   b) People can only change themselves.
   c) If I cannot change others, I should change something in myself.

2a) I have no influence on these people

The 1st axiom of WATZLAWICK (in HOBMAIR, 1997) says: 'In a social situation one cannot not communicate'. This (non-provable) theory contains that even to ignore a communication or other people holds a communicative character, as e.g. 'I don't like that' or 'I don't agree to what you said'. Thereby there is always an influence.

2b) People can only change themselves

As a rigorous solution-oriented human being, who encourages independent competence for solutions, this view may suit the acceptance of individual responsibility and the believe of self-effectiveness. In most cases we decide for ourselves what to do how.

Although there are two facts against the view that other people can only change themselves: environmental influences, memorised in an archive of internal rules difficult to reach by our consciousness, e.g. rules our parents taught us which strongly influence our way to approach solutions. And according to the rule 'the being determines the consciousness' we adjust to e.g. people's images, how we work or dress. The direct influences by other persons or advertisement via the media has more influence on us than we would have thought or believed.

The 2nd aspect emphasizes the systems view: without the conversation with a solution-oriented listener I would probably never be able to use the solutions I have within myself. Even if I do not learn any new things, the solution-oriented conversation can encourage and help me to change my view.

2c) If I cannot change others, I should change something in myself

Whenever people meet, different norms, values, rules, perception and needs meet. These differences will release the striving to convince the others to take over ones own views. The background herefore is the inner rule: 'I feel good, if you do, assess and think this, if I do, assess and think thus' or 'I am better than you are'. In a performance-oriented society and especially amongst men this rule is widely spread.

Mostly such a motivated process of convincing comes over as nagging, spoiling the atmosphere and worsening the relationship, as the needs for respect and self-realisation of one party are ignored.

But there is only one way to co-operative solutions: Both want it! If you notice that, even after years of training he/she does into change, it seems more worthwhile to concentrate your reserves, stay calm and to accept what apparently cannot be changed. If your solution for a problem is not achievable, set new goals! Maybe it is more difficult to work on oneself than other people but your chances of success will be even bigger. Systematic thinking integrates both views of the interactions to a trouble-free whole. The being has an influence on the consciousness as also the consciousness has an influence on the being. Therefore, thesis 2a) and 2b) can be dismissed.

Cognition 8:

Solution-oriented people integrate suggestions and stimulations into their lives and use new as well as successful reliable ways to reach their goals.

Mistake 9:
To give too much significance to unpleasant thoughts and feelings!

Whenever problem-focussing people feel uneasy they look for explanations and causes. To find the cause attribution helps to reduce unpleasant feelings and moods. Although no solution ideas or attempts have been made. In problem-focussing thinking associates unpleasant situations to further unpleasant incidents, then again worsening the emotional state. To brood over incidents we cannot change any more, to evoke catastrophes that will never happen and a good portion of self-pity often robs our energy for the change.

We could use the same energies more positively, if we would recall successes and imagine our goals as really appealing, they would drag us closer in reality. The belief to be able to manage the conflict situation successfully can be strengthened with the ability to dream.

Solution-oriented people use thus time and tell themselves: OK if that is the problem, which solutions could be there, which alternatives have I got? This opens the exit out of the problem view. Thenext step is to imagine what it would be like if everything went smoothly: 'What would it look like? What will I say and do? How will I feel?' Dreams are thoughts full of strength. During the night daytime conflicts are worked over. Use your dream energy and allow yourself a 'dream holiday' from the waking state! Look at things, places and persons around yourself in the condition after you have reached your goals. What will you do and enjoy if you are in this condition? What will have changed and how will you feel if things are such that you have solved your problems?

Cognition 9:
Use the strength of your phantasy and regularly imagine the condition of your live after the miracle has taken place.

Mistake 10:
If something goes wrong, just carry on ...

EYSENCK's cognition at the beginning of the book is the call for changes. To keep the good and change the bad is an essential part for satisfaction, contendness and effectivity in the working and personal life.

The keep/change technique offers you the possibility to check the way things stand for yourself as well as for your relationship, your team and your system.

Which three things would you like to keep?
Which three facts would you rather change immediately?

The replies to the second question hold the entrance into a solution-oriented discussion. Within groups a consent should first be found over what everybody and what oneself wants to manage. This working in the solution world avoids endless talks about what supposedly cannot be done and creates a creative mood of learning. Although the 1st rule of change remains the demand to change.

Cognition 10:
If something does not work, do something else!

∽

Solution-orientation in thought and action is a basic stone to reach inner contendness. It activates your own abilities in a plesant atmosphere. Conflicts can be solved saving time and symptoms caused by problem-focussing like the inner notice of employment or somatic complainst like sleeping problems and circulatory disorders, stomach pains and headaches as well as general aggression and agitation can be noticably reduced.

The ABC of change offers the structure and accompanying questions, which will strengthen your solution-orientation. You can use these abilities for yourself and also in your dealings with other people. Solution-orientation always also means customer-orientation, also means to respect your colleagues and to keep conflicts small. You will learn to value this effect. Try it straight away and think opimistically about the pleasant effects, the return of the smile.

V. 9 QUESTIONS AND 9 ANSWERS

1. What has the concept 'resilience' to do with solution-orientation?

Resilience means the psychical and physical strength which lets people manage any life crisis without any reduction in the long run. Innate facts like intelligence or vivacity as well as environmental factors like a sound emotional relationship, social models for a constructive solution-finding and to cope with past achievement demands increase the resistance. Resilient people appear like boxers who try a different tactic in the ring after a knockdown:

'Change something if things do not run as they should!' According to WHITE (in NUBER, 1999) you will then avoid two basic mistakes:

Mistake 1: You are cursing your crisis –
And put all attention to it.

Mistake 2: You feed the crisis in that you pay full attention to the problem and its emergence but do not consider the question how to solve it.

According to psychological research (NUBER, 1999) resilient people with a well-developed personality factor have the following features:

- You accept the crisis and the attached feelings,

- Resilient people look for solutions,

- Resilient people do not feel a victim, who often use phrases like 'I cannot', 'I will never be happy again' and so on,

- They will not solve their problems on their own:
  they will use their family and friends and avoid big talkers,

- Resilient people remain optimistic: They are sure that things will change to the positive sooner or later.

This should not be mixed up with positive thinking, which denies reality and wants to flatter negative incidents,

- resilient people do not blame themselves,
- resilient people plan ahead: They ask the 'what if …'-question.

Solution-orientation and resilience are two almost identical concepts; resilience emhasizes the resistence in crisis, whilst solution-orientation describes ways to solution in daily thinking, speaking and acting. Solution-oriented communication offers a training program for readers to enlarge their own solution-orientation together with their resilience and to help others to strengthen their resilience.

2. How good does the principle of solution-orientation work?

In all my coaching meetings where I used solution-orientated communication, I received a positive feed-back to the procedure in every respect. The awakening of the inner energy and the revived believe in one's own abilities was described as especially valuable. I found it astounding to observe the high rate of success in reaching the step-by-step goals. Memorised knowledge from the short term consultation report an average period of 3.5 hours where classical therapies with an identical rate of success needed at least 5 times as long.

3. How can the solution-oriented start be so effective?

A large part of the time is used for the productive work with solutions. The transfer from a problem-discussion into a solution-discussion already happens during the 1st meeting. Tasks regarding the relevant situation accelerate the awareness of thoughts, feelings and behaviour as well as the experience of successful incidents.

4. Solution-oriented communication – what is its biggest advantage?

Every weekday psychologist, so every person can easily learn it. It is a well-formed structure of questions and memorised experiences, which broadens the palette of individually available abilities to lead a discussion and the ability to change and help to structure it. To acquire a solution-oriented discussion-basis has the advantage that you:

- can use everywhere,

- can always disgress solution-oriented and at the same time know that there are still questions to be asked to transfer yourself or others into the condition of reaching the goal.

You only have to exercise to ask solution-oriented questions instead of problem-focussing ones and to change your own way of thinking.

5. What is the biggest disadvantage of this start?

There is a time to moan and a time to act. Whoever did not get so far as to articulate and approach his/her goals will find him/herself in Part 1 of the book (problem-discussion). The ability of ones partner to listen attentively and persistently are extremely important. If you are more interested in the past, in the 'why' things have developed as such there are other proceedings (like thepsycho-analysis).

6. Your image of human beings?

In such a complex world of various cultures and generations the amount of hits of the same images would be minimal. I believe that all people can improve their life style by changing their inner rules, thoughts and view on solutions instead of focussing on problems.

7. Is this start useful for small and medium companies?

The start is very useful for companies of any size, as it is the point to put one's knowledge, experience and energies into the company and not to be blocked by 'Nos'. Disappointments have to be overcome and changes forced into being. The more solution-oriented you communicate the more you automatically reach your customers and colleagues, as you establish a pleasant atmosphere on the relationship level. Nowadays this is a crucial factor in advertising!

8. Where in Germany can one learn solution-orientation?

In Germany there are more and more advisors, trainers and coaches who use solution-orientation. I would advise you to look in the internet for the terms solution-orientation and coaching. You will surely find some information under HYPERLINK "http://www.MarcusStobbe.de".

9. How do solution-orientation and neuro-linguistical programming stand to each other?

Comparing neuro-linguistical programming and solution-orientation with each other, the following mutualities and differences can be found: Both procedures have the goal to leave problem-focussing and to react flexible to all difficult situations in life. Both procedures evaluate the valuable experiences of the past more than traumatic experiences. Both prefer the short-term treatment as in most situations one strives to leave the problem fixation to mobilise existing reserves and to recover the ability to act.

The neuro-linguistical programming combines elements of the stuy and communication with psychological experiences. Contrary to this solution-oriented communication combines the solution-oriented start with the behavioural start of the problem description.

The solution-oriented start offers the opportunity to integrate methods used by the neuro-linguistical programming as a tool. Solution-orientation is a start that records what works. As people find their own solutions (again) during a conversation, diagnosis, drawers and archiving are unnecessary and blocking: what would it help to know that somebody is an alcoholic or cause-oriented, where this illness originates? It seems more interesting to be able to do other things instead of drink alcohol and to activate the necessary abilities.

∼

VI. LITERATURE

BAMBERGER, G. G.: *Lösungsorientierte Beratung.*
Weinheim: Psychologie Verlags Union, 1999.

BANDURA, A.: *Social foundations of thought and action: A social cognitive theory.* Englewood Cliffs, NJ: Prentice-Hall, 1986.

BUCHNER, D.: *Team-Coaching: Gemeinsam zum Erfolg.*
Wiesbaden: Gabler, 1995.

CUELHO, PAULO: *Der Alchimist.*
Zürich: Diogenes, 1996.

DREES, A.: *Folter: Opfer, Täter, Therapeuten. Neue Konzepte der psychotherapeutischen Behandlung von Gewaltopfern.*
Gießen: Psychosozial-Verlag, 1997.

EPSTEIN, D., WHITE, R.: *Die Zähmung der Monster,* 1994.

FARELLI, F., BRANDSMA, J. M.: *Provokative Therapie.*
Berlin: Springer, 1986.

GARDNER, H.: *Dem Denken auf der Spur: Der Weg der Kognitionswissenschaft.* Stuttgart: Klett-Cotta, 1989.

GORDON, T.: *Manager-Konferenz.*
München: Heyne, 1989.

GORDON, T.: *Die neue Familienkonferenz.*
München: Heyne, 1989.

GRAWE, K., DONATI, R., BERNAUER, F.: *Psychotherapie im Wandel: Von der Konfession zur Profession.* Göttingen: Hogrefe, 1994.

HENNIG, C., EHINGER, W.: *Lösungsorientierte Beratung.*
Beckmannweg 16, 72076 Tübingen.

HOBMAIR: *Psychologie.* Köln: Stam, 1997.

HUCKE, H.: *Wer früh' aufsteht, wird reich: Lebensweisheiten.*
Köln: Buch und Zeit, 1997.

Latane, B.: *The psychology of social impact.*
American Psychologist, 36, 1981.

Lay, Rupert: *Dialektik für Manager.*
München: Langen-Müller/Herbig, 1994.

Mehlmann, R., Röse, O.: *Das LOT-Prinzip.*
Vandenhoek & Ruprecht, 2000.

Montamedi, S.: *Ein harter Schlag – Provokative Kommunikation.*
in: ManagerSeminare 5/6, 1999, 58-64.

Nuber, U.: *Das Konzept ‹Resilienz›: So meistern Sie jede Krise.*
Psychologie Heute, 5/1999.

Reeve, C.: *Immer noch ich. Mein zweites Leben.*
München, 1999.

Satir, V., Banmen, J., Gerber, J., Gomori, M.:
Das Satir-Modell. Paderborn: Junffermann, 1985.

Shazer, de Steve: *Wege der erfolgreichen Kurztherapie.*
Stuttgart: Klett-Cotta, 1995.

Shazer, de Steve: *Der Dreh.* Heidelberg: Auer, 1997.

Sprenger, R.K.: *Das Prinzip Selbstverantwortung.*
Frankfurt/Main: Campus, 1998.

Thurmaier, F., Engel, J.: *Wie redest Du mit mir.* 1995

Zajonc, R.B.: *Feeling and thinking: Preferences need no inferences.*
American Psychologist, 35, 151-175, 1980.

Zimbardo, P.G.: *Psychologie.* 5. Ausgabe, Berlin: Springer, 1992.